OZARK
GHOST STORIES

NOMINEE

SOUTHEASTERN
LIBRARY
ASSOCIATION'S

SOUTHERN BOOK COMPETITION

1994 / 1995

OZARK
GHOST STORIES

Collected and Edited by
Richard and Judy Dockrey Young

August House Publishers, Inc.
LITTLE ROCK

Published 1995 by August House, Inc.,
P.O. Box 3223, Little Rock, Arkansas, 72203,
501-372-5450.

Printed in the United States of America

10 9 8 7 6 5 4 3 2 1 PB

LIBRARY OF CONGRESS CATALOGING-IN-PUBLICATION DATA
Ozark ghost stories /
collected and edited by Richard and Judy Dockrey Young.
p.   cm.
Includes bibliographical references.
ISBN 0-87483-410-4 (pbk.) : $9.95
1. Tales—Ozark Mountains.
2. Ghosts—Ozark Mountains.
3. Ghost Stories, American—Ozark Mountains.
I. Young, Richard, 1946- . II. Young, Judy Dockrey, 1949- .
GR108.3.093   1995
398.2'09767'105—dc20   94-41669

Executive editor: Liz Parkhurst
Project editor: Rufus Griscom
Design director: Ted Parkhurst
Cover art and design: Wendell E. Hall

*The editors wish to dedicate
this collection to the memory of
Vance Randolph (1892-1980)
and Miss Mary Celestia Parler (1904-1981),
former professors at the University of Fayetteville.*

The paper used in this publication meets the minimum requirements of
the American National Standard for Information Sciences—Permanence of
Paper for Printed Library Materials, ANSI Z39.48-1984.

AUGUST HOUSE, INC.   PUBLISHERS   LITTLE ROCK

Preface

"EVERY HILLTOP HAS ITS TRADITION, every hollow is full of tales and legends."* With these words folklorist Vance Randolph described the Ozark Mountains of Arkansas and Missouri in 1957. It was true in the early 1800s when these hills were first settled permanently and in large numbers by pioneers from Europe, and it is still true today as tourists from around the world beat a path—or follow an old one—to the Ozarks to enjoy recreation in woods and on lakes, preservation of crafts and folkways, and celebration of American country music. One of the folkways practiced in daily life, and preserved in the tourism industry, is Ozark storytelling.

While many different kinds of storytelling abound, from narratives sung in ballad form to simple narrative jokes, the most popular tales are stories of the supernatural. The term "ghost story" encompasses many varied types of stories from witch lore to monster yarns, only some of which involve the spirit of a departed person.

This collection spans the same broad range, from the "Ballad of Floyd Edings" to the popular ghost joke "Stealing

---

*Randolph, Vance. *The Talking Turtle* (New York: Columbia University Press, 1957, page xv).

Pawpaws," from the witch tale "The Cat's Paw" to the traditional Ozark monster known as "The Gowerow in Marvel Cave."

At this writing, we live along the Old Wilderness Road (now called Highway 13) in Stone County, on Nickerson Ridge, in the little community now called Stoneridge. It was on this very ridge that Tomp Turner saw the headless ghost he described to Otto Ernest Rayburn. If it was Old Raw Head, he's been in our front yard . . . but not recently. All we've seen so far is deer. But the stories linger on.

These are the stories still told around campfires and at fishing lodges, still heard on long automobile or school bus trips, and still recited around a fireplace or a lit candle at Halloween and Christmas. These are our favorite Ozark ghost stories.

As Randolph said, "The finest yarns were spun by the flicker of log fires."

—Richard and Judy Dockrey Young
Stoneridge, Missouri
All Hallows' Eve, 1994

Contents

V. Truthful Tales

VI. Haints and Hollers

VII. Ghost Jokes

Appendices

Introduction

—STORYTELLING AND THE OZARKS—

IN ALL THE EARTH, the most beloved form of folk entertainment is storytelling. It connects us to our prehistoric ancestors in the Old World who gathered around cave wall paintings to recite the lore of the clan; it joins us with all other cultures on our planet today, for all of us share the oral narrative as an integral part of our heritage. Literally everyone knows and tells stories, even if they are only the terse distillations called jokes.

Many Americans think that storytelling is a dying art because it is absent from their hi-tech, modern lives. But in areas of the world where technologies are parallel to, or even secondary to, more traditional ways of life, storytelling flourishes. Of course, Bedouin tents in the Sahara are such a place, as are grass huts in the South American jungle, but there are also regions of the United States that maintain traditional folkways alongside modern technologies. Surely we have now all seen on television the careful maintenance of traditional crafts, folk arts, folk music and storytelling in the Appalachian Mountains, where a satellite dish casts a shadow on a front-porch banjo picker and kids turn off the laser disc to ask Grandpa for a ghost story. There is another, less well-documented region of America where traditional storytelling is observed: the Ozarks.

Geologically speaking, the Ozarks are low hills and knobs. Knobs form the same way mesas do, but the capstone top has a rounded mound of soil above it and deep drainages in an uplift called the Ozark Plateau. The Plateau covers northwest Arkansas and south-central and southeast Missouri. Culturally speaking, the Ozarks Region, where traditional folkways and storytelling still thrive, is a much larger and less well-defined area.

Within this broad region (defined in greater detail in the following section) lie the Ozark Mountains, the St. Francis Mountains and the Courtois Hills in Missouri; the Ozarks, Bostons and Ouachitas in Arkansas; the Kiamichis, Sanbois, and the Cookson Hills in Oklahoma; and the Ozark foothills in northeast Oklahoma and southeast Kansas. The inhabitants of these hills are primarily what we jokingly call the "Midwest Mix": Scots-Irish, English, German and American Indian. And that's all in one family, mind you! Each of the cultural heritages represented honors storytelling, and we find it a vital part of daily life.

Who tells stories in the Ozarks? Everyone—except for some city residents who have forgotten how. In the rural and agricultural areas, especially in the backwoods, storytelling is still very popular. It was, of course, even more popular before radio and television were commonplace in Ozark homes, but these modern conveniences came late to some regions of the hills. For example, Arkansas 7 from Russellville to Harrison— more than eighty miles along some of the most scenic hills and valleys in the state—was not paved until 1947. Just off that venerable road lies the little town of Ben Hur, named for the Lew Wallace novel popular in the 1890s, to which electric lines were not run until 1968! (Madison County, west of Scenic Highway 7, has its seat at Huntsville, and was in 1994 still without a traffic light anywhere in the county.) The slower pace of life and the late arrival of electricity and coaxial cable or satellite dishes helped prolong the popularity of storytelling.

Storytelling today is still favored as the amusement of choice on long automobile rides, and on school bus trips that wind through dark hollows coming home late at night from ball games in the nearest town with a comparable school rating—sometimes as much as a hundred miles away. Fishermen sit on gravel bars around a fire at night on float trips, hunters sit on logs around a campfire under the autumn stars, and Halloween party-goers sit around a fireplace or a lighted candle: these are favorite places for tall tales and scary stories. Television, VCRs, books and comics *have* replaced storytelling in many situations, even in the Ozarks, and bedtime stories are less common now than in previous decades when every Ozark child was tucked into the covers with a tale. But in other situations storytelling has transformed as times change. Where once the village loafers and retired gentry hung around the blacksmith's shop and the horseshoe pitching pit exchanging yarns, they now sit on park benches in the city square endlessly whittling and chatting. ("Been working on this one a few weeks, it's gonna be a toothpick for my granddaughter.") In homes, family storytelling may be restricted now to holidays and reunions, instead of being told every night, and stories told at bedtime may be the plot-lines of remembered cartoons mixed in with more traditional tales. Professional storytellers performing at theme parks or visiting in schools may carry more of the burden of preserving and perpetuating the art than do the hill folks themselves today. But yarnspinning, even the telling of anecdotes instead of full-length stories, brightens the day and passes the time during repetitive chores like snapping beans or family gardening. As a result, even in this decade, stories are exchanged and shared during family chores done while seated, during work in the family garden by two or more generations working together, and in similar situations. Same-generation storytelling is still shared around the wood stove in the general store that many communities still have, as well as in the kitchen during family gatherings. Skip-a-generation storytelling still takes place at grandpa's knee or grandma's lap. And child-to-child storytelling is still common on the school bus, playground, or at slumber parties or "sleep-overs." Storytelling now is not as common as in previous decades, but it is alive and well as a folk art form.

In the Ozarks, men and boys have traditionally told stories about what a fool some other fellow is, about outlaws of days gone by (from Jesse James to Bonnie and Clyde), about ghosts, and about hunting, fishing, and sporting. Women have traditionally told fairy tales, folk tales, folklore and superstitions, and family lore. Women traditionally do not tell ghost stories, and refrain from telling jokes in mixed company, but that is gradually changing with time. Grandparents feel free to tell any genre of story, especially to grandchildren, in their role as the main preservers and perpetuators of the traditions of their individual families and of the local culture (especially of the "good old days"). We have observed that, to one degree or another, everyone loves to hear and tell one kind of story in particular: the ghost story.

There are certain problems in putting any Ozark story down on paper, which we will present later, but there is also a slight difficulty in the very act of naming "ghost stories." The word *ghost* implies the spirit of a departed human being, which is the customary belief of northwestern Europe, from which the majority of our Midwest Mix ancestors came. Ozark residents define *ghost* in about the same way as other U.S. citizens of similar ancestry, but to an Ozarker a ghost story may tell about a ghost, a ghoul (returned from the grave in physical form), a witch, the Devil himself, a fantastic monster (such as a gowerow, a jimplecute, a tantarabobus or a wompus cat), a spook light, a booger (undefined supernatural evil creature) or booger animal (a sort of spirit animal, usually larger than life and unkillable), or a blight (an evil spell cast by a witch or witch man, or any evil force that frustrates and destroys hope).* Stories in this collection represent all the various supernatural and preternatural beings covered by the generic Ozark term "ghost story."

Finally, by way of introduction to these narratives, we must point out that "story" means different things to different people. Some folks tell only ghost jokes, others tell only sketchy summaries of longer narratives heard in their youth. In fact, we often gather stories one piece at a time from different informants who remember different fragments and leave different lacunae ("holes" or omissions in a story variant). As these lacunae are filled, a story takes shape that does not come from a single individual.

The narratives in this anthology are the most common in the Ozarks, the ones we have heard told the most, and the ones we are most often asked about. For further information on the boundaries of the Ozark region, the history of Ozark storytelling collection, a comparison of folklorists' methodology to those of storytellers, and an explanation of how we collected these stories, read on in this introductory article. For the great ghost tales themselves, turn to page 26!

—THE BOUNDARIES OF THE OZARK REGION—

As we survey the region, the Ozarks are bounded as follows (and a good atlas may be necessary to trace the boundaries).

---

* The word *blight* is of unknown origin, according to *Webster's Dictionary*, and we are inclined to believe it is a very old pre-Christian word among the Anglo-Saxon English. We have used this term even though its use in the Ozarks today is almost nil, and not well documented.

Beginning at the headwaters of the Little Osage River northwest of Old Fort Scott, in southeastern Kansas, the northern edge of the Ozarks region runs along the drainage of the Little Osage into Missouri, then along the drainage of the Osage to the Missouri River at Jefferson City, and along the southern bluffs of the Missouri River loess to its confluence with the Mississippi (excluding metropolitan St. Louis).

The eastern boundary is harder to plot. Beginning with the confluence of the Missouri and Mississippi, the boundary follows the western bluffs down the Mississippi to Sainte Genevieve, then along the foothills past the confluence of the Whitewater and the Castor to Poplar Bluff. Following the foothills into Arkansas, the boundary runs along the western banks of the Little Black and the Black Rivers to Newport, and down the White River, then back up Cypress Bayou toward Lake Conway and across the Arkansas River around Mayflower.

Here many Ozark scholars trace the southern edge along the north banks of the Arkansas River to Oklahoma. We have found that the folkways and storytelling traditions extend farther southward, and our view of the regional boundary carries it southwestwardly along the foothills of the Ouachita Mountains following Interstate 30 from Little Rock to Benton, the area just south of and along U.S. 70 through Hot Springs to DeQueen, and into Oklahoma to Broken Bow. Taking in the Kiamichi Mountains, the boundary turns northward up the drainage of the Little River.

The western boundary is ill-defined, culturally and geologically. From the bend in the Little the boundary runs northward through Nashoba, Tuskahoma, and up Oklahoma 2, in foothills and up the lakes system of the Neosho (or Grand) River from Old Fort Gibson to the Kansas state line. In Kansas the boundary runs up the Neosho, but seems to travel up

Lightning Creek to its headwaters, and across to our starting point near Old Fort Scott. (In Kansas, the prairie way of life predominates west of the Lightning, even though the state road system identifies the Ozark Pioneer Trail out west of that stream.)

There is still one tiny island of Ozark-like culture that is not within these boundaries, but which we have identified through many pleasant visits with the locals. The bluffs area of Illinois, along the eastern bank of the Mississippi, outside the large urban areas, in Madison, St. Clair, Monroe and Randolph Counties proudly maintains some of the old "hill folks" way of life.

—THE COLLECTING OF THESE STORIES—

Judy was born in the Ozark foothills at Muskogee, Oklahoma, and lived at Wagoner for many years, moving deeper into the Ozarks to Rescue, Missouri, in grade school. Her extended family came from the hills of South Carolina and has lived in Oklahoma since long before statehood, and she has heard hill stories all her life. Her father's favorite story was "Stealing Pawpaws" (page 163).

Richard was born in the low Texas hill country, at Huntsville, to a family that has roots in the hills of Giles County, Tennessee, since shortly after the Revolutionary War. Richard's family moved to Winslow, Arkansas, in the Boston Mountains, in junior high school. Living in several Ozark cities (Siloam Springs, Fayetteville, and Harrison) through three decades, he has heard hill stories all his life, and constantly adds to his collection of ghost tales. His father's favorite story was "The Hainted Car" (page 166).

From our family backgrounds, we moved into storytelling and performing at Silver Dollar City, a nostalgic 1880s theme park west of Branson, Missouri, Judy in 1978 and Richard in 1980.

These stories were collected:

- In the daily family lives of the editors since early childhood.
- Between 1959 and 1968 at storytelling sessions in Siloam Springs and at the University of Arkansas at Fayetteville;
- Between 1973 and 1979 at storytelling sessions among the cast of Dogpatch USA, a theme park south of Harrison, Arkansas;
- Between 1979 and 1992 at Halloween parties and other ghost storytelling sessions in Harrison, Arkansas; and
- Since 1980 in story sharing in connection with performances of storytelling at Silver Dollar City, Missouri.

When storytellers gather, it is customary to "trade off" tellings; at ghost storytellings, everyone in the circle usually takes a turn. In this way, we have heard the stories assembled here varying numbers of times. Over the years we have developed distilled versions of each of these stories, which represent the most typical way we have heard each one told (rather than a single variant as told word for word by one informant).

We have chosen for this collection the stories we have heard most often, and the stories which are most tellable and most pleasing to audiences. There are many old standards, known across the English-speaking world, as well as some purely Ozark yarns that shed light on Ozark ways. Some of these stories come from far outside the region, but Ozarkers always take a story they like and salt it to their own taste.

Because good stories are kept alive through telling in the Ozarks, most of these stories have been around a long, long time. Most have been collected by folklorists Vance Randolph and Otto Ernest Rayburn and appear in one form or another in their books. In some cases, the stories we heard told must have been passed down orally over the last century; in other cases, we suspect the stories were read in Ozark books, and re-entered the oral tradition through retelling. (We have observed this with our own books; a youngster will tell us a story he read and learned from "a book," and ask if we know it. We smile, realizing it was one of our books. We show him the book and his eyes get large.

The final decision on which stories to include in this collection was based on these criteria:

- Tellability; we have had the benefit of years of storytelling stage time and audience reactions to judge which stories "tell" well.
- Audience/Reader appeal; these are the stories we are most often asked to tell or retell by audiences and other story listeners.
- Regional Representation; these stories represent Ozark heritage well, without requiring massive explanation or footnotes.
- Enjoyment; these are stories we enjoy ourselves.

We have deliberately omitted many fragments, some stories that are scatological, any story wherein the explanation was longer than the narrative (hill folks understand them fine; flatlanders don't), and stories which more readily fit into another category (e.g., tall tales, jack tales, etc.).

In our collecting of stories in the Ozarks, we were preceded by two giant figures in the grassroots folklore movement, and a brief summary of their lives' work follows.

—OZARK FOLKLORE PIONEERS—

Otto Ernest Rayburn (1891-1960) was born in Bloomfield, Iowa, and educated at Baker University in Baldwin City, Kansas, Drury College in Springfield, Missouri, and at the University of Arkansas at Fayetteville. He collected stories while editor of *Ozark Life Magazine* at Winslow and at Kingston, Arkansas, and later as the editor of *Arcadian Life Magazine* from Caddo Gap, Arkansas. (The name refers not to ancient Greece but to the scene of rural peace and simplicity Rayburn found in Arkansas.)

Rayburn's great Ozark work (he wrote many volumes of poetry as well) was *Ozark Country,* and he and Vance Randolph were friends and collaborators in the collection of tales and Ozark folklore.

Vance Randolph (1892-1980) was born in Pittsburg, Kansas, in the very edge of the Ozarks, and educated at Kansas State Teachers College and at Clark University. He worked collecting stories as assistant state supervisor of the Federal Writers Project in 1936-37, and as a free-lance writer thereafter. He first visited the Ozarks proper in 1899, and lived here almost continuously after 1920. While quietly writing fifty books and pamphlets, he lived among the hill folks and learned their ways. He was one of them, one with them, and his friendship and kinship with the folks always took precedence over the collection of lore. He lived out the last years of his life in Fayetteville, where these editors knew him.

Rayburn's major work, and Randolph's best-known works, are further described in the Bibliography on page 187.

—A COMPARISON OF FOLKLORE
AND STORYTELLING METHODOLOGIES—

Folklorists record or preserve a single variant of a story at a time, with all the lacunae and imperfections of the specific teller, along with many details about the teller that reveal the cultural context and delve into the meaning of the story within that culture. Storytellers are more content to collect the story as a body of variants, incorporating them into a single, distilled version of the story that represents the culture that tells it.

When folklorists preserve a story, it is like a dried butterfly in a case: a perfect example of something that was once alive, captured in great detail for future generations to enjoy and study. As storytellers, our interest is in a living story that remains alive as it is retold, and that changes with time as tellers and listeners change.

Folklorists have a captive audience in the future generations and current researchers who will seek out their collections. Most storytellers (except for those in cultures where story-telling is a formalized ritual and storytellers do not rely on audience support for their living) have to select stories that will benefit specific audiences, and present those stories in ways that those specific audiences can understand and appreciate.

Folklorists are very careful not to retell stories, but preserve them; they are careful not to allow any part of themselves to enter into the story. A storyteller, on the other hand, realizes that each teller adds a little of himself or herself to the story, even tellers in the story's culture of origin. A storyteller will try to tell the story in such a way that it is faithful to its culture but also faithful to the audience and the art form. We, as collectors, editors, and storytellers do not make a conscious effort to alter the stories we tell; we also do not fear the natural processes by which stories evolve and are pleased to present these stories to a wider audience of readers and retellers.

—ELIZABETHAN EXPLANATIONS FOR GHOST SIGHTINGS—

The speech and customs of the Ozarks are not Elizabethan, but many archaic traditions and anachronistic phrases survive in the Ozarks that outsiders often consider Elizabethan. In Shakespeare's time there were four theories on who was most likely to see a ghost. Shakespeare accommodated all four theories in *Hamlet*, and all four explanations are still offered by different Ozarkers today to explain why some people see ghosts and others do not. Often the reader will see one of these as pertinent to a story in this collection.

Those most likely to see a ghost are those who:

- have recently suffered the loss of a loved one (as Hamlet's loss of his father),
- are considered insane (as Hamlet feigns, or perhaps is),
- are closer to nature and farther from cities or technology, perhaps less educated (as the guards on the castle wall who first see Hamlet's father's ghost), and
- inhabit or visit the site of a wrongful or unprepared-for death (as is the castle of the King of Denmark in *Hamlet*).

Hill folks who do not believe in ghosts, and some who do, offer one of the above explanations for the sighting of ghosts by their neighbors.

—NOTES ON COLLOQUIAL OZARK SPEECH—

The speech of Ozark hill folks has become more like standard

English in recent years, with television and radio influence in homes in the last half of the twentieth century, but there are still old-timers and even some young folks who have learned the traditional speech habits. Sometimes these speech habits only emerge in the telling of traditional tales. As a result, these editors have heard renditions of the texts collected in this anthology in varying levels of grammaticality and have presented the stories as closely as possible to the way we first heard them.

For readers not accustomed to Ozark speech, we offer these notes:

Many Anglo-Saxon words, pronunciations, and patterns of speech persist in the Ozarks. The suffix "-ly" on adverbs and some adjectives is replaced by the older "-like," (natural-like," "frightened-like") resembling the Old English "-lice," akin to the German suffix "-lich."

Double and triple negatives are normal, as they were in Chaucer's day, with the number of negatives increasing the strength of negativity.

Subjects are often restated, as in "Pa he called to us."

The short phrase "and all" is used for emphasis and in place of the phrase "et cetera." One hears "what with her being poor and all," and the expression "still and all" to mean "nevertheless" or "in spite of it all."

The verb "was" often replaces "were" in statements; conversely, "were" often replaces "was" in questions. The pattern, generally, is to use "was" in statements and "were" in questions.

Past participles are often used in place of the simple past tense, even when the resulting word is longer than the correct word. One hears "taken" for "took," "run" for "ran," "come" for "came," and so on.

Archaic words like "offen" for "off," "iffen" for "if," and

"et" for "ate," still found in unabridged dictionaries, are heard occasionally.

Archaic constructions like "may be" (short for "it may be that ...", pronounced as two distinct words) used in place of "maybe" and "Do tell!" (short for "And do you tell me so!") used in place of the Midwestern "Well, how about that!" are common as well.

One aspect of Ozark speech that we have deliberately omitted for the sake of clarity is regional pronunciation. Heard aloud, these stories would contain the phonetically-rendered "chimbly" for "chimney," "painter" for "panther," "bile" for "boil," and many other regionalisms. See our "Notes on Ozark Dialect" in *Ozark Tall Tales* (Little Rock: August House, 1989), page 15.

—PROBLEMS PUTTING OZARK STORIES ON PAPER—

The following groups of problems face the story collector who attempts to put Ozark folktales and other narratives down on paper.

You can transcribe the words, but *not*

- the vocal and manual sound effects (growls, finger snaps, hand claps, etc.)
- the facial expressions and body language (sneers and grins, leaning toward the listener, folding the arms, etc.)
- the changes in the pitch, tone, timbre, or emotional quality of the voice (changing from character to character, keening, droning, etc.)

In some stories the above elements comprise fifty percent of the total information of the story (i.e., 50% verbal and 50% body language).

Ozark vocabulary, pronunciation, and phraseology are different from those of standard English. To reach a much wider audience, a great deal of the regional "color" has to be standardized, and part of the "charm" and even the content is lost.

Many Ozark stories contain subtextual references to superstitions, taboos, and other kinds of shared cultural traditions not well known or understood outside the Ozarks. These nuances are lost on the average reader.

Ozark folkways contain many elements that require explanation to the uninitiated. Some stories we know would require an explanation longer than the text of the story. (e.g. "He lit a shuck outta there" is used to mean "he left in great haste and desperation." It refers to the use of a fast-burning, twisted corn shuck as a candle. On a trip to the outhouse on a dark, moonless night, the unlit outhouse is an impossible target without the shuck lit from the fire, matches and candles being too expensive to waste on so simple a purpose. A barefoot local who may also be superstitious and fear the dark or the night—two separate fears—would not make the trip in the dark, so the shuck is an absolute necessity and the trip is made in haste. Once inside the privy, one finds one's way by feel, and for the trip back to the cabin, the lit windows or open door give one something to walk toward).

Finally, Ozark humor tends to be so subtle, and so often deliberately "concealed" from "furriners" or "flatlanders" (see the Glossary, page 169) that it is lost on the average reader ("The Cat King" page 93 is a good example).

In cases where the problems given above reduce the quality and value of the story substantially, we have chosen to omit the story rather than give an unsatisfactory or "hollow" rendition. As to the other stories, whose impact is lessened by these problems, but which we have included in this anthology nevertheless, we believe they will stand on their own. For the best rendition, these stories should be read aloud, or told from memory, ideally by an experienced Ozark teller!

I. STONE-COLD FAVORITES

These graveyard yarns are the epics of Ozark ghostlore.
These are the tales we hear the most, are asked to tell the most,
and those that bring out the most spirited response.

OLD RAW HEAD

(RAW HEAD AND BLOODY BONES I)

DEEP IN THE OZARKS, folks have always known that there were conjurin' women who knew the use of roots and herbs for medicines, and the use of "remedies" and spells. But there was witches, too, bad witches that had to be avoided, or laid low with good witchcraft when there was bad witchcraft afoot.

One ol' woman was a conjurer, but she wasn't such a bad type; she often used her spells and remedies for good. She had a familiar spirit, the ghost of a dead witch man, that came to her in the body of an old, wild razorback hog, and he helped her with her spells.

One October, at Halloween, the folks in the valley was holdin' a' early hog-scaldin'. Every October the hill people would slaughter hogs and put up the meat into the smokehouse for the long winter. When the wind blows cold and the frost comes and the leaves turn, it's hog-scaldin' time. Men gather from miles around, and drive their hogs into rail-fenced pens. The animals are slaughtered, and the carcasses scalded enough to get the bristle hair off. Then the butcherin' begins. By sundown, the meat is all packed in burlap sacks to go home, and the raw, skinned hogs' heads and the bloody bones are all that's left out from those burlap sacks of meat.

One old, lazy hillbilly *stole* hogs from his neighbors at

hog-scaldin' time, and one year he must've rounded up that conjurin' woman's familiar, too. After the butcherin' that day, he rode away with a bag of meat and a skinned hog head in the back of his wagon. But the wagon wheel hit a bump, and out onto the dark road rolled the old raw head.

"Bloody bones," said the old raw head, "get up and dance."

The bloody bones back at the butcherin' pens jumped up, and danced around, and pulled themselves together again, and came and got the head.

Old Raw Head ran into the woods and went to all the critters and borrowed things to wear. He borrowed the panther's fangs; he borrowed the bear's claws; he borrowed the raccoon's tail. And he went to the house of the lazy hillbilly who stole the hogs.

The old man and the old woman were in bed when they heard a scrabblin', clatterin' sound, and sparks jumped offen the coals in the fireplace. The old man got up to see what was the matter. He looked and looked and looked, and couldn't find the intruder. Then, he looked up the chimney.

"Land o' Goshen!" said the old man. "What've you got those big old eyes for?"

"To see your grave!" said a deep, hollow voice up the chimney.

The old man ran away.

A minute later he came back, and looked up the chimney again.

"Land o' Goshen!" said the old man. "What've you got those great, big claws for?"

"To dig your grave!" said the deep, dark voice.

The old man ran away again. But a few minutes later he came back and looked up the chimney again.

"Land o' Goshen!" said the old man, "What've you got that big, bushy tail for?"

"To *sweep* your grave," said the rumbling, rolling voice.

The old man ran and hid under the bed and from there he said, "Land o' Goshen! What've you got those long, sharp teeth for?"

"To *eat you up!*"

At that, Old Raw Head came down the chimney and grabbed the lazy thief and ran out the front door with him. You could hear the old man a-hollering and a-screaming 'way off in the woods.

The next morning, a party of men set out to find him.

Old Raw Head had stolen the lazy hillbilly's horse, and they tracked the horse to Hog Scald Holler. There they found a fresh pile of unnaturall' large, bloody bones. But no head at all.

At night, in the full of the moon, Old Raw Head rides the stolen horse through the hills and hollers of the Ozarks and holds his old skinned raw head in his hand … high up against the moon!

RAW HEAD AND BLOODY BONES II

(Also known as LITTLE JOHN NUMBER EIGHT)

ONCE UPON A TIME there was a little boy named John, who was the eighth child in the family. He was called Little John Number Eight. Little John was a rascal; he never did mind his mama and he always went out of his way to get into trouble. It just came to him natural-like. Even the scariest threat of all didn't unsettle his ways.

Little John Number Eight was a handsome one, but his looking good didn't fit to the way he behaved. He was a mean one, and he never listened to the old folks or the truth they tried to teach him about. But still his dear mama loved him ever so, even though when she'd tell him not to do something, he'd go right on ahead and do it anyways. He sure was contrary and ornery, that Little John Number Eight.

"Now, don't you go steppin' on no toads," his mama would say to him, "or it'll spoil the milk our cow gives."

"I promise, Mama," Little John Number Eight would say, "I won't step on no toad frogs." But as soon as he was down the lane and out of sight, he'd run to the first toad he'd see and jump right up in the air and come down and squish that toad. Why, iffen he could've, he'd've squished him a whole bucket-full of toad frogs.

And sure enough, the old cow would give sour milk. And his mama would shake her head, but she loved him ever so.

"Now, don't you go whistling at the dinner table or singing in bed," his mama would say to him,

"Whistle at the table
or sing in bed,
and Raw Head and Bloody Bones
will see you dead!"

"I promise, Mama," Little John Number Eight would say, "I won't whistle at the table or sing in bed." But when he was at the table and everyone else was outside, he'd whistle up a storm, and iffen he was in bed and all the rest of the family went out to feed the stock late, he'd sing like a whole church choir, only they wasn't songs you'd want to be heard singing in church.

But nothing came of it at first, so he got bolder, and he went to stepping on crickets, too. Pretty soon his little sister had the bellyache and his whole family couldn't earn any cash money. And all because of him. But still his mama would just shake her head, because she loved him ever so.

"Don't you get to moaning on Sunday or groaning on Monday," said his mama, talking about slacking away from church and school,

"Sunday moans and Monday groans,
will bring Raw Head and Bloody Bones!"

"I promise, Mama," Little John Number Eight would say, "I won't moan on Sunday or groan on Monday." But pretty soon, when Sunday rolled around, he commenced in to moaning about going to church and washing behind his ears and all. He laid out from church, pretending to be sick. It worked so well, he began to practice his Monday groans, so as he could lay out of school.

Sure enough, as Little John Number Eight sat at the table, just whistling away, with all the family at church, he began to groan out loud just like he'd do the next morning. Then he thought he heard something up the chimney groaning, too, and he got real quiet.

But since nothing came of it, he just laughed after a minute or two and went out and stepped on some toads.

But sure enough, that Sunday night, in the dark of the moon and the still of the night, while Little John was practicing his groans for Monday morning, up from the grave and into the cabin came Raw Head and Bloody Bones.

When Little John groaned in his bed, up the chimney groaned Old Raw Head.

When Little John got up to see what the noise was, he lit a candle. Out of the chimney came Old Raw Head, and in the flickering of the candle, Bloody Bones squished Little John Number Eight into just a grease spot on the table.

Then the candle went out.

The next morning, Little John's mama was up early and taken a wash rag and wiped up that spot and said,

"I must've missed that spot after supper."

And that was the end of Little John Number Eight; and that's what happens to all bad little children who never mind their mama.

THE WOMAN IN THE BED

ONE TIME A FELLER from in town was travelin' the back roads
to see his shirttail kinfolks, and it was a three-day walk, so he
stopped off at a cabin where he saw a light burning. He wanted
to see if he could pass the night at their place. He knocked on
the porch post, and someone inside called out for him to come
in. Inside, a fire was lit in the hearth, but there were no
lanterns.

Three men was playin' cards at a table by the fire, and they
was dressed particular' strange', like folks was inclined to dress
in olden times. They hardly took notice of the traveler as he
came in. He stood there for a minute or two, shifting his
weight from one foot to t'other, and finally spoke up when no
one ever spoke to him.

"Can I pass the night here with you'uns?" he asked.

For a long time none of the men spoke. Then one of them,
who was smokin' a clay pipe, looked up kind of sudden, like
he's just heard the traveler come in, and he said, "You sleep in
the bed, there, if you like, but don't wake the woman there.
She mustn't be bothered. It's a long trip for us tomorrow, same
as for you."

The man hadn't said he ought to pay anything, so the traveler thanked him, and walked to the bed. He took off his shoes
and slipped quietly into the covers on the side of the bed nigh

to the fire. The woman under the quilts didn't move or say anything. The traveler was so tired he fell right to sleep, not bein' used to walkin' that far in a day, and all.

He 'woke with a start some hours later. The fire had died down, and the gamblers was gone. With the fire down to just coals, the cabin was deadly dark. One shaft of moonlight come in through a crack in the shutters, and the traveler could see the woman still in bed.

He sat there for a moment, then slowly leaned over to her to lift the covers and look at her pretty face.

She didn't have a face.

She'd been dead for days, and dogs had been chewin' on her face and hands. As the man screamed and rolled outten the bed, the woman rolled after him, like she was comin' to get 'im.

He grabbed his shoes and ran for the door a-screamin', and there was a sound behind him like somethin' heavy hittin' the floor.

He went to the nearest settlement and got the constable. But when they come back to the cabin, it was cold and empty, and had been for years. The hearth was swept clean and covered in a layer of dust. The furniture was gone and the shutters were off. There was an empty rope bed frame in the corner. The bedding was long ago rotted into a pile of straw and rag on the puncheon floor.

"Crazy city feller!" mumbled the constable as he left.

The traveler went home and wrote to his cousins that they could come and see *him* next time.

PENNYWINKLE! PENNYWINKLE!

A YOUNG WOMAN BORE A SON, but died shortly afterwards. Her husband buried her in the graveyard, and found a widow woman with a young daughter and asked her to be his wife. She accepted, and the two came to live in the cabin, but the stepmother hated the baby boy that wasn't hers. She never mistreated the boy in sight of his father, but when the man was away, she was *mean* to that boy.

As the boy grew older, she hated him all the more. She wished he'd die, so her daughter would get all the care in the household. That spring the man bought a suckling pig and brought it home to fatten in a pen. When the woman got mad at the boy, she'd go outside and beat the pig! She dasn't beat the boy for fear the man would find out.

One day the man said it was time to butcher the piglet, and he went out to plow in the bottom land a far piece away. While he was gone, and the young daughter was to school, the mean woman went out to butcher the piglet. She opened the pen, but the shoat feared her so by then that it squalled and ran between her legs, out the gate, and into the woods. She couldn't find the pig, and dasn't explain why a pig would run from food.

She called the young boy out to the pen and hit him in the head with the maul, like she'd've done the pig. She cut his throat and bled him out. Then she butchered the boy like he was a pig, and cooked up the meat. Her man didn't favor hog liver, so she put the liver and lungs and the goozle and windpipes into a flour sack along with the head. When her daughter came home she said, "Take this sack of parts and bury it under the broken marble cooling stone out by the shed. I don't want no flies, nor no dogs dragging pig innards around the houseyard."

The daughter did as she was told, and had to struggle to lift the slab of marble. When the sack was buried, she dropped the slab back into the hollow it had made over the years, where pennywinkles bloomed around it.

When the father came home, he asked about his son.

"Your boy went to sassing me, and when I spoke sharply to him, he run out the door and swore he'd never come back," said the woman.

"I've got to go look for him," said the father.

"Set and eat first," said the woman with an evil smile. "Then we'll all go."

After they'd all et their fill, the woman said she couldn't go out after all, she was having a sick spell. She packed another flour sack with cooked meat for the man. He told the daughter to stay behind with her mother. He took the sack of meat and biscuits and set out to look for the boy.

The mother went right to bed and began to have nightmares. The daughter blew out the lamp and went to sleep on her own bed after a while. Deep in the night she awoke to a small, clear voice, saying,

> *"Pennywinkle! Pennywinkle!*
> *My ma killed me, my pa et me;*
> *And my sister buried me beneath the slab!*

I want my liver and lights and whiny pipes!
Pennywinkle! Pennywinkle!"

She knew that little voice! As she sat up a little pile of pennywinkle flowers fell from her chest. Knowing what had happened, and what she'd done, she looked over at her mother in the darkness. The mother didn't stir, and didn't seem to hear.

The girl got up and put on her shoes, and grabbed her shawl and ran out the door as quiet as she could. She ran and ran down the holler to find her stepfather. The man had searched and searched and called and called, but couldn't find his son. He'd sat down under a willow tree and et some of the meat and biscuits, planning to sleep a spell, and get back up an go to searching again.

As he slept, he had a dream. He heard a small voice call to him,

"Pennywinkle! Pennywinkle!
My ma killed me, my pa et me;
And my sister buried me beneath the slab!
I want my liver and lights and whiny pipes!
Pennywinkle! Pennywinkle!"

The man sat bolt upright.

And a little pile of pennywinkle flowers fell off his overalls' bib. He knew what had happened, and what *he* had done.

Just then, his stepdaughter came running through the trees in the moonlight calling to him. He grabbed her and hugged her hard and they told each other what they'd heard.

"I was so scared," said the girl. "I ran to you to help me." They started back to the cabin through the dim, brushy woods. The woman stirred in her sleep. And the voice called to her,

"Pennywinkle! Pennywinkle!
My ma killed me, my pa et me;
And my sister buried me beneath the slab!
I want my liver and lights and whiny pipes!
Pennywinkle! Pennywinkle!"

She sat up in the bed. The cabin was black as sin. Something stood at the foot of her bed.

The father and the daughter ran into the houseyard. The father took up the axe from the chopping block. They came slowly into the dark cabin.

The woman was in bed and did not stir. The father held the axe up as the daughter lit the lamp from a sulfur match.

The woman was on the bed with her eyes wide open. Her throat was cut, and she had bled out all in a pool that ran down the mattress and dripped on the wood floor. In her right hand she held her butcher knife, clotted with her own blood.

In her other hand she crushed a handful of pennywinkles.

BLOOD-RED CEDAR

ONCE THERE WERE A YOUNG MAN and a young woman who got married and lived in a house on a hill. The woman brought with her a hope chest made out of blood-red cedar. In it she kept her linens and things, where the moths wouldn't hurt them. When her first child was born, it was a little boy. His skin was as white as linen, and his healthy lips were as red as blood-red cedar. They named the boy Will.

When Will was a boy, his mother died of a fever. Will's father knew he couldn't raise the boy alone. He married a widow woman who had a younger daughter named Marjorie. Will and Marjorie loved each other like brother and sister, but Marjorie's mother hated Will and wished he would die.

One day there were apples picked fresh and brought into the house. Will came in from chores and wanted one. The evil stepmother took him to his mother's blood-red cedar chest to get the silver knife to peel the apples with. When Will bent over to reach into the chest, the stepmother slammed the lid.

Will's head fell off into the chest.

The stepmother laughed and laughed, but she knew she would have to hide her crime. She set Will up in a chair in the kitchen and set his head on properly. Then she tied a napkin around his neck as if he were about to eat. She put an apple in one of his hands and the silver knife in the other.

When Marjorie came into the house, she saw the apples. She asked if she could have one. "Share your brother's apple," said her evil mother. When Marjorie asked Will for a piece of his apple, Will did not answer. "Just hit him, then," said the evil woman.

When Marjorie hit her brother, his head fell off, and Marjorie thought it was her fault. She cried and cried. Now, the woman said she would hide Marjorie's crime, even though Marjorie had not killed her brother.

The woman cooked Will in a pot and served him for supper. She told Will's father that Will had gone away to live with an aunt. Only Will's father ate that night. Marjorie only cried.

After supper, little Marjorie gathered up all the bones, wrapped them in her linen napkin, and buried them under the red cedar tree in the yard. A strong wind blew and the cedar tree shook.

Then the cedar gave off its red powdery pollen as if it were springtime. The red powder whirled around the tree in the wind. It looked as if the tree were on fire. It looked as if the tree were red with blood. The tree shook, and a little bird flew out of its branches. The bird landed in another tree and began to sing.

> *My mother, she murdered me.*
> *My father, he ate me.*
> *But my loving sister Marjorie*
> *Put all my bones beneath a tree.*
> *And I came back to sing on high.*
> *Oh, what a pretty bird am I.*

Marjorie laughed and clapped her hands. She knew that the bird was her brother. There was magic in the cedar tree.

Marjorie went back into the house.

The pretty bird flew over the fields and forest and into the village. The bird landed on the window of the metalsmith's house. The smith was forging a chain of silver to take to the fair and sell. The bird began to sing.

> *My mother, she murdered me.*
> *My father, he ate me.*
> *But my loving sister Marjorie*
> *Put all my bones beneath a tree.*
> *And I came back to sing on high.*
> *Oh, what a pretty bird am I.*

The metalsmith looked up. "That tune is the most beautiful song I have ever heard. If you will sing it again for my wife, I will give you this silver chain."

The bird agreed. The smith called his wife, and with their arms about each other, they listened to the song. The smith put the silver chain around the bird's neck.

The pretty bird flew over the houses and roofs and landed on the window sill of the bootmaker's shop. The bootmaker was making a fine pair of boots to take to the fair and sell. The bird began to sing.

> *My mother, she murdered me.*
> *My father, he ate me.*
> *But my loving sister Marjorie*
> *Put all my bones beneath a tree.*
> *And I came back to sing on high.*
> *Oh, what a pretty bird am I.*

The bootmaker put down his tools and said, "That is the finest song I ever heard a bird sing. If you will sing it for me again, I will give you this fine pair of boots."

The bird agreed and sang the song again. Even though the boots seemed quite large, they somehow fit the little bird perfectly, and he flew away.

The pretty bird flew over the river and over the millpond and landed in the window sill of the grinding mill. Men were just finishing putting in a new stone to grind the corn. The old millstone, as round and flat as a giant's pancake, sat against the wall. The bird began to sing.

My mother, she murdered me.
My father, he ate me.
But my loving sister Marjorie
Put all my bones beneath a tree.
And I came back to sing on high.
Oh, what a pretty bird am I.

All the men agreed that the song was the most unusual one they had ever heard. They asked the bird to sing it again. "If only you will sing that song again, we will give you the old grindstone from the mill. You can build your nest in the hole in the center."

The bird agreed and sang again. The men lifted the grindstone. Though the stone weighed many pounds, the bird put its head through the hole in the center of the stone and flew away with it.

The pretty bird flew to Marjorie's house and sat above the front door. He began to sing.

My mother, she murdered me.
My father, he ate me.
But my loving sister Marjorie
Put all my bones beneath a tree.
And I came back to sing on high.
Oh, what a pretty bird am I.

Marjorie knew it was her brother singing, and she ran outside. The bird bowed its head and the silver chain fell off. It fell around Marjorie's neck and made her even prettier than she was before.

The father heard the bird singing, and he came from the barn. The bird picked up its feet one by one and kicked off the boots. When the boots hit the ground, they were just the right size to fit the father's feet. He took off his old boots and put on the new ones.

The evil stepmother came up from the root cellar to see what bird was singing.

Marjorie and her stepfather told the evil woman about their gifts. She asked the bird, "What have you brought for me?"

The bird bowed very low, and the heavy millstone fell from its shoulders. It fell on the evil woman and crushed her.

The bird flew down to the millstone. When he landed, there was a burst of fire, or of cedar pollen, or a splash of blood. There was Will, standing on the millstone, well and whole.

Will told them both what had happened. The three lived happily. And when Will's father married the miller's sister later, she was a kind and loving stepmother to them all.

BLOOD IN THE ROOT CELLAR

ONCE AN OLD WOMAN was in a rush to fix supper for her man, for she'd been gossipin' with her neighbor over the fence rail, and the sun was nigh onto settin'. She sent her pretty daughter to the root cellar to fetch some potatoes for the soup. The girl skipped out to the cellar and climbed down the steep stairs into the dark.

It was dusky-dark inside, and one beam of sunlight came in the ventpipe and shone by the potato pile. The girl knelt down to pick up some of the potatoes in her apron, and she saw this little pool of blood on the dirt floor. She sat and stared at it for a moment, and a little voice said,

"... if you tell your mother about my blood ... I'll come and *get* you ..."

The girl jumped up and ran back to the house and told her mother.

"That's just tomato rot, you silly girl," said her mother. "Get back down there and bring me them potatoes!"

The little girl went down the steps again. They were steeper than before, and the cellar was darker. The beam of light shone on the pool of blood, and now it had a head growing out of one end of it with two little black eyes. The head looked at her and said,

"If you tell your mother about my head ... I'll come and

get you ..."

The girl ran out of the cellar and told her mother what she'd seen with the little black eyes.

"All potatoes've got eyes, child," laughed her mother. "Now get down in that cellar and get me them potatoes!"

The girl went back to the root cellar and back down the stairs. Only now they were steeper and there were more of 'em than ever before. The beam of light shone on the pool of blood, but now it had a great big body growing off the other end of it, with little hands and feet getting bigger all the time.

"If you tell your mother about my body, I'll come and *get* you!" it said. "Now pick up your potatoes and *get out!*"

The girl grabbed up a load of potatoes and ran outten the cellar as fast as she could. She took the potatoes to her mother who peeled 'em and boiled 'em and thought no more about it. The girl didn't say anything about the thing-in-the-root-cellar's body.

She just et her supper and went on to bed.

At midnight the fire gave a *crack!* and the girl awoke.

Something big and black and heavy walked slowly across the cabin floor towards her. It stood beside her bed in the darkness for a long, long time. Then it slowly laid its big hand on the girl. She felt its claws touch her ever so lightly.

"If you had of told your mother about my body ..." it whispered in a deep, growling voice, "I'd've come and *got* you."

The thing patted her ever so softly and turned away.

The floor creaked as it walked to the door and out into the night. The thing pushed the door slowly to, and she heard the latch drop into place here inside.

She was kind of used to the thing by now, and she wasn't scared a bit.

THE DUMB SUPPER

EVERY YOUNG GIRL wants to know whom she's going to marry, and there are several ways of divining who it'll be. One way is to boil an egg, peel it, and cut in half crossways. Then lift out the yolk and fill the half with salt. Eat that half and go to bed thirsty. In your dream, someone will bring you a drink. Whoever brings the cup is the one you'll marry. If a member of your family brings the drink, it means you'll be a spinster.

But the best way to find out who your intended is, is to hold a dumb supper. A young girl who seeks to know her future husband's name gathers two or three of her girlfriends together and they begin to make the dumb supper.

First of all, no one speaks from the time the preparations are made until the supper is eaten, and that's why it's called a dumb supper. While making the preparations, the girls do everything as backward as they can. One girl stands facing away from the table and kneads the bread dough behind her back, and so forth.

When the meal is all cooked, the girls go silently to some private place, especially an empty outbuilding or a cabin that's nearby but deserted. Barring that, at least they go to some house other than the house of the girl who wanted to know. And it is best if you could actually prepare the meal at that other house or deserted cabin.

When the meal is served, the girls sit down and eat in silence, and supposedly someone else comes and eats silently with them. That person will be the future husband of the girl holding the dumb supper.

Now, I suppose that when girls held dumb suppers in the past, one of the girls usually sneaked away and told the boyfriend of the girl holding the dumb supper so he could show up and eat with them in silence. But the superstition went further than that. People believed that the ghost of the living person destined to be the husband of the girl left his body and came to the dumb supper so that the feller could be reported as seen somewhere else while his ghost was there eating in silence.

One day a group of girls got together, and one of them who already had a boyfriend, but wanted to be sure they were destined to marry, said she wanted to hold a dumb supper. They stood with their backs to the kitchen cupboard as they did all their cooking, they didn't say a word from the minute they began to cook the meal, and when it was ready they packed it in baskets to take to a deserted house just down the road.

In those days, when somebody moved, they just left the house open and empty, leaving behind the furniture they had hand-built, knowing they could hand-build some more when they got to wherever they were going. A lot of the land was of questionable ownership anyway, being sold and resold at auction for back taxes, so folks just settled where they felt like and stayed a few years before moving on. About all they'd take with them in their wagon when they left was the cedar chests and the camelback trunks their clothes were kept in. If you couldn't get it all into a trunk, you probably didn't need it anyway. Folks just had their clothes they had on, and their other clothes for Sunday, and that was about it.

Anyways, the girls walked to this abandoned house and turned the table upright, and put out the dumb supper. They found things to sit on, and began to eat silently.

In the course of the meal, the boyfriend of the girl who was holding the dumb supper came up to the house and came in and laid his pocketknife down at her place at the table. Not a word was said. Then, he left in silence without partaking of anything, just to show that she was his and he was hers. That knife was a prized possession, and so she knew how sincere he was.

Not many months passed until, sure enough, those two got married. Things went along well for about ten years after that, but then they had some bad times and he took to drink. One evening he came home drunk and found her going through her trunk, looking for something that she needed. Just as he came along, she took the pocketknife out of her hope chest.

He looked at her real rough-like and said, "I always wondered what happened to that knife ..." and he took it from her and opened the blade.

He stabbed her to death with it.

It *had* been his ghost at the dumb supper, and not him.

RACHEL AND THE GOLDEN COINS

AN OLD MAN PUT BACK A GOLDEN COIN EACH YEAR, hidden in a flour sack, buried in a mason jar. The older he got, the richer he got, but he died before he could spend it, or even tell anyone where he had hid it. He died sudden-like, alone in his cabin up on Yokum Creek in Missouri.

Neighbors found him and buried him in a pauper's grave, and his furniture was put up for sale to pay the undertaker. The house sat empty for a year or so; it wasn't on good land, and no one felt like paying the back taxes on it. Finally, an orphan girl named Rachel came into the county and set up housekeeping at the empty cabin on Yokum Creek.

There wasn't any furniture except for the bed frame, which was made in one corner of the room by nailing boards along two walls out of a corner, and connecting them by nails with two boards that sat at their corner on a single bed leg cut from a tree trunk. Over that four-board frame was woven a rope bedspring. All Rachel had to do was gather armloads of cornshuck and stuff a mattress she made by sewing together two old unfinished quilts she had brought with her.

The first night on the bed, where the old man died, she was sound asleep when a cold hand brushed her forehead. She jumped up and looked around in the dim glow off the fire coals. There was no one there.

The day went by well enough, and Rachel did some planting in the old garden.

The second night was like the first. Deep in the night Rachel felt a cold hand lightly brush her forehead. This time she opened her eyes but didn't get up. She looked slowly around the room and saw nothing. The fire still had one glowing ember, and she could see around the place fairly well. She was all alone in the cabin.

The next day went by tolerabl' well, and Rachel swept the house out good with a twig broom she made from some buckbushes.

The third night she slept with her head to the corner of the room, instead of out toward the fireplace. In her church, it didn't matter which-a-way you slept; toward the east for Judgment Day, or not. With her head to the corner, she could see the whole room just by opening her eyes. She went on to sleep the same as always, but she took her only butcher knife to bed, and laid it alongside of her under the covers.

Deep in the night a cold hand brushed her forehead, and she opened her eyes while it was still touching her.

There was a shadow leaning over her, touching her lightly on the forehead. It wasn't a person, just the shadow of a person, that blacked out part of the starlight and all of the glow from the fire. The shadow stood slowly up, as if looking at Rachel. She sat up slowly and smiled her friendliest smile.

"What in the name of the Father, Son and Holy Ghost do you want?" she asked it.

The shadow pointed out the door. Rachel got up, and took the knife in her hands, and hid it under her shirt, just in case. She walked to the door and opened it. The shadow went out beside her, and all she could see was just a darkness where it was, and all she could hear was just a cold wind that brushed past her with the shadow.

The shadow walked out to the chinaberry tree in the front yard. Rachel followed it. The shadow bent low and pointed to the ground at the foot of the tree. Then it stood back up and turned toward her as if waiting. Rachel just stood there, not knowing what to do. The shadow leaned toward Rachel and pointed at her shirt, where the knife was hidden, and then bent down and pointed to the ground at the foot of the chinaberry tree.

Rachel knelt down and stuck the knife in the ground just at the foot of the tree. When she stood up and looked for the shadow, it was gone.

The next morning Rachel went out to the old shed and found the rusty blade of a shovel. She dug in the earth where the knife stood. Two feet down she found a half-gallon Mason jar with a rusted lid. In the jar were a hundred gold coins.

FINGER BONES

IN THE HILLS, there was a haunted house that sat at the edge of a ridge. It stood two stories tall, and had a cupola with a weather vane. The cellar was unnaturally deep, being built into a limestone cave. The house was home to an old widow woman, who was cared for by her granddaughter in her declining years. After the old lady passed on, the granddaughter was there alone for a few months. Then the granddaughter vanished, and the house stood empty for years.

Soon, the folks 'round about began to see a ghostly light in the parlor of the house, and some of the menfolk went up to see about it. The house was empty, all right, but there was still some furniture in it. The men sat around with a low fire lit in the hearth. At midnight the door from the basement swung open and a young woman came out.

She was dressed in a long dress, but it was rotting away. Her face was that of a corpse, with much of her flesh rotted away. The men jumped up and started to run, but she cornered one and took ahold of his lapels in her rotting hands. She was just about to speak, when she faded away like a mist.

By morning, her hand print had rotted through his coat, and his shirt showed. The men were waiting outside the preacher's house when he came out to the well at dawn to get water. They explained what had happened, and he agreed to spend the night in the house and try to help the tortured soul find peace.

That very night, the preacher man was seated in the chair in the dark, dusty parlor, with another low fire burning in the hearth. He had his pocket watch about him, and he knew when midnight was nigh.

At the stroke of midnight, the door from the cellar swung open, and up the stairs came a rotting corpse of a young woman. She came straight at the preacher, and raised her hands as if to grab him by the lapels. The preacher raised his Bible slowly up and asked,

"What in the name of the Lord do you want?"

The figure broke apart like mist and faded from sight before she reached him. He sat back down in the chair.

At the stroke of one, the door from the cellar swung open, and up the stairs and into the parlor came the rotting corpse. She came straight at the preacher as he slowly stood. She reached out her hands as if to grab his coat lapels. He raised the Bible high and asked, "What in the name of the Lord do you want?"

The hands turned to mist and the body soon followed, wavering like a reflection in running water. Then she was gone.

At the stroke of two, the door from the cellar swung open again, and up the stairs came the hideous, ghostly figure. The preacher stood sooner and raised the Bible higher, but he waited until she was right in front of him, and her bone-and-gore hands closed about the lapels of his frock coat.

He looked her straight in the eyes, and said,

"What in the name of the Lord do you want?"

"My jularky murdered me," she said, in a horrible, bubbling voice. "Take the bones of my little finger and put them in the offering plate. They will point out the one who killed me.

Then let him be brought to trial. When he is punished, come back to my cellar."

Recognizing the young woman, the preacher said,

"You were to be married in my church. I know you were planning to wear your grandmother's wedding dress. In my church you shall find justice and peace for your soul."

She slowly released her grip on his lapels, and then she took one hand in the other, and broke off her little finger. She dropped the bones into the preacher's waiting hand, and then she wavered like someone seen through the flames of a campfire, and she broke apart and was gone.

But the bones remained in the preacher's hands, and he put them loose in the offering plate that Sunday night at church. Outside the church, in a cold evening mist, stood a white figure in a wedding gown. Inside, by the light of the lanterns, the offering plate was passed from hand to hand as the pump organ played the offertory hymn.

Suddenly one young man, a fancy dresser and ladies' man, let out a scream. He held up his hand, and the bones were gripped around it like a finger again, like a hideous wedding ring. The offering plate hit the floor and the coins rolled all over the church. The young dandy was screaming and tearing at his hand, and confessed everything as the congregation slowly gathered around him in a circle.

The young dandy was hanged the next day, and buried. The men from the church went into the cellar and found the body of the murdered girl and carried it all in a sack and buried it, too. The last man to leave the cellar was the preacher, and as he started to leave, the light of his candle reflected off something under the stairs.

There was a steel box with a shiny lock, which he carried to the church and opened. Inside was enough gold to provide for the needs of the congregation for many a year to come. The preacher and his family moved from their little cabin into the fine, two-story house, and cleaned it all up, and made it the parsonage.

And never again did the cellar door open at midnight.

VANISHING RIDER

ON A COLD, WINDY NIGHT, a young man was riding alone on a dark road in the hills. The moon was full, and it was the corn-shockin' moon. As he rode along, the sound of the horse's hooves echoed off the cliff face through the brush to one side of the trail. All sudden-like, he saw a young woman standing beside the trail, dressed in a calico dress, but without even a bonnet on to keep her warm. The boy thought that her horse must have thrown her and run on home without her. Or maybe she had walked too far from the house at dusk and lost her way.

He rode up beside her and said, "Evenin', Miss. It's a cold night out for a young lady without her bonnet."

"Evenin', Sir," she said. "Could you give me a ride to my rightful place?"

She sure was pretty, and didn't seem to mind the cold at all. Now in those days a young man going courtin' would ride to the young woman's cabin, leading a saddled horse of his along for her to ride. If she didn't ride good, he'd lead her along from on his own mount, but iffen she was a good rider, she'd just ride alongside him to a play party or to a dance. So this young man had never rid' with a young lady on the same horse before, and he was plumb nervous about it.

"Sure thing, Miss," he said. She put her foot on his boot and reached up for his hand, and then smiled. He hoisted her up, and she rode astride the horse behind him, on the tail of the saddle blanket. He took off his own scarf and passed it back to her to wrap her shoulders in. She put the scarf on, and reached around him and hugged him tight.

And she said with a smile in her voice, "I'm set."

The young man goaded his horse, and they started down the trail at an easy jog. As they rode the young man couldn't think what to say to this beautiful girl. And she held him closer than ever, as if to keep warm. She laid her head against his strong back and said, "It's a lovely night."

"Sure is," the young man managed to say. Her arms around him felt so good, but she seemed awfully cold, and he wondered why her teeth didn't chatter. He let go of the reins with his right hand, and folded his arm over her arms to keep her warm. She sighed and snuggled up against him so lovin'-like that he reached his hand into her hand.

And they rode on holdin' hands for a while 'til they come to the buryin' ground.

"I'll get off here," she said sweetly.

Well, the boy couldn't figure out why. He didn't recollect there bein' a house anywheres near the graveyard. May be her family was travelin', and they had camped for the night under the brush arbor. Before he could say anything else, she put her hand on his shoulder and slid down to rest her shoe on his boot. As she was steppin' down she looked him in the eyes and smiled at him sweet-like, and kissed him on the cheek.

"Thanks for the ride," she said. She was so graceful and so beautiful; she was off the horse and walkin' into the graveyard toward the brush arbor, out of sight, before he realized that she was still wearin' his scarf.

He sat there for a moment, then slapped the reins on his horse and rode home fast. The next mornin' he was up with the chickens and out of the cabin before daylight. That there scarf gave him the perfect excuse to go and see her again. He rode up to the buryin' ground just as the sun was comin' up.

He dismounted beside a buggy that was tied there, and lookin' into the graveyard he saw a man standin' in the midst of the stones, dressed in a long frock coat. May be it was her pa. The young man tied his horse aside t'other one, and walked into the buryin' ground.

"Mornin', Sir."

"Mornin', young fella."

All a-sudden-like, the boy recognized the older man.

"You're the judge, ain't you, Sir?"

"Yes, I am," said the man.

Having hoped to meet the family of travelers and seein' no one else around, the boy thought that the judge might know something.

"What brings you to the buryin' ground so early?"

"I've come to visit my daughter's grave," said the judge. "She died seven years ago last night, in Indian summer. Her horse threw her. It was down the road about a mile, there." He pointed back along the cliff side, and then turned and stared at the gravestone in front of them.

The boy felt a cold chill, even though the sun was hittin' 'im now. "I met a girl last night ..." he said. And then, for the first time, he looked down at the gravestone.

"You're the seventh boy that's given her a ride home," said the judge, with a tear in his eye. And he bent down and lifted the boy's scarf off the gravestone where it lay wrapped around the corners of the marble. "Here, son, you'll be needing this back."

The judge walked away and the boy stood there for a long, long time before he climbed on his horse and rode back home again.

PETIT JEAN

HIGH ABOVE THE ARKANSAS RIVER stands Petit Jean Mountain. On its southeast overlook is a tiny grave surrounded by a rusting iron fence. People who live in the valley below often see lights hovering around the grave late, late at night. Some say it's just kids or tourists; the rest know it's what the Indians saw for years before the valley was settled. It's the ghost of Petit Jean.

When the French explorer Chèves set sail from Calais in France to come to the New World, he left behind his fiancée Adriénne. Just before he sailed, a new cabin boy signed on, a youth with a lovely face. The boy followed the troupe up the Mississippi, and up the Arkansas. They stopped near the present town of Morrilton.

A little settlement was built with log houses, and the friendly Indians of the area were fascinated with the mysterious boy. They saw in him features of both man and woman, and considered this to be a sign of spiritual gifts. His name was Jean and people called him "Little Jean."

When Chèves announced that he would return to France and bring his fiancée back to this pleasant land, the cabin boy asked to go, too. When Chèves refused, the lad fell very ill. While caring for the lad, the Indians learned the strange truth. They told Chèves the cabin boy was Adriénne, who had followed him in disguise.

Chèves rushed to her side, but she died in his arms, telling him that she loved him and this place and these Indian people. She was buried atop the escarpment, and her ghost walks the cliff edge still as the beautiful Little John, "Petit Jean."

II. BOOGERS AND BLIGHTS

Whether giant or spirit animal, graveyard ghoul,
terrifying apparition, or the Devil himself,
"booger" is the Ozark word for it.

MARY CALHOUN

ONCE THERE CAME TO THE OZARKS from Ireland a family by the name of Calhoun. The eldest child was the daughter Mary, the apple of her father's eye. And one day, passing through the graveyard on the top of the hill near the house, the father of the family stopped to rest on a sarcophagus and watch the sun go down. When he got up and walked on, the old man was so refreshed that he forgot his walking stick.

At the house, where the supper table was all but laid, he mentioned his walking stick, and Mary said she'd go back and get it, and be to the house again in a shake. Out the door she went before anyone could stop her.

Entering the graveyard, she walked toward the sarcophagus her father had mentioned, and there she found the walking stick leaning up against the stone. She bent down to pick it up, and noticed in the moonlight a broken-down grave at her feet. It was an old grave, and it had been dug shallow, as if those who dug it were in haste, or as if there was no family to remound the grave when the coffin inevitably collapsed and the grave caved in.

As she stood there staring fixedly at the cracks in the ground, a bony white hand reached up out of the grave and grasped the hem of her dress!

She started to let out a scream, but she found she could

not.

Out came another hand, and grabbed her dress higher up. And slowly something very, very old and dead climbed up her garment until it sat on her shoulders.

"Walk!" said the thing, in a voice like wind in dry autumn leaves.

And Mary Calhoun walked against her will, held in thrall by the power of the thing. Down the lane they went, towards the houses along the path, beyond the fallow field. The thing on her shoulders was light, like husks at shucking time, but it was also heavy with the weight of unspeakable evil, buried in the cold earth for a century or more.

"I'm hungry!" said the thing. "For I've not et in many a year. Turn in here," said the thing at the first house.

Then, "No! Turn away, there's holy water in this house."

At the next house, "Turn in here."

Then, "No! Turn away, there's holy water here, on garments blessed at mass!"

At the third house, "Turn in here."

Then, "Go in, for there's no holy water in this house."

Inside the house, Mary found that all the family, neighbors whom she knew well, were fast in bed. Somehow time had flown for them but crawled for her as she had stared at that broken-down grave.

"Go to the kitchen!" the thing said.

She went, all unwilling.

"Get a knife and a bowl."

She got as she was bidden.

"Upstairs," the thing pointed as it spoke.

She went up, with the thing a-riding her shoulders.

In the loft slept three fine sons of the family, Mary's childhood playmates.

"Cut their throats," said the thing.

And with trembling hands and tears in her eyes, Mary cut the boys' throats. When the first drop of blood fell into the bowl, each boy stirred. With the second drop, each boy grew cold and still. With the third drop, each boy was ashen and dead.

Mary took the blood in the bowl, and returned to the kitchen.

"Make gruel!" said the thing.

And she did. When the water was boiled and oatmeal and the blood poured in, the thing commanded:

"Serve us!"

Mary took two bowls and spoons from the cupboard, and napkins from the dry sink, and the bowl of bloodied oatmeal from the stove, and set the table.

"Now, take a morsel!" the thing bade her.

Mary's hand shook as she lifted the spoonful of the horrid gruel toward her mouth. Her hand shook so violently that she dropped the bite into her kerchief at her neck, where it could not be seen. The spoon went on up to her lips, her jaws worked, and her throat swallowed, all against her will.

"Now that you've et in the house of the dead, you're one of us!"

The thing climbed slowly down, and sat at the table, unaware that Mary had not eaten the morsel! When the thing had let go of her garment, its power over her faded away. But Mary was a clever lass, and sat down stiffly, and pretended to eat as if the spell still held her.

As the thing slavered and drooled and ate away at the bowl of gruel, Mary lifted spoonful after spoonful towards her mouth. And when the thing was not looking, she dropped each bite into the folds of her kerchief at her breast. When both their bowls were empty, the thing stood up and said, "We'll leave now."

"I'll take up first," said Mary, and she took the bowls, the serving bowl, the spoons and the napkins to the dry sink in the kitchen. She took off her kerchief, folded it over the gruel in it, and set it in the dry sink. When she returned to the parlor, the thing climbed her dress again and sat on her shoulders.

The powerful spell returned and Mary did as it bade her: "Back to the graveyard."

And they went out onto the path and passed the houses, towards the fallow land.

"Now you're one of us," said the thing, "you can know what the dead know. That gruel made you one of us, but if any had been left and fed to those dead boys, why, they'd rise up alive again."

A little further along, the thing said, all chatty-like, "That cairn of stones there, under it I hid all my gold ill-gotten in life. But little good it did me."

Back in the graveyard, Mary saw the sun was about to rise. Time had flown again as they ate their gruesome meal. The thing climbed down and Mary felt the spell fading away.

"Come down, Mary Calhoun, into your new home," said the thing.

"I'll not come down!" cried Mary. "For I've et none of your hideous gruel!"

The thing let out a terrible oath and started to climb back out of its grave and clutch at her dress.

The sun rose over the hill, and sunlight struck the thing. Mary grabbed her father's walking stick and flailed at the thing. The thing flew into a thousand sparkling shards like husk or vellum, and the sun rose over the graveyard.

Mary took her father's walking stick and started home.

She turned in at the third house, where the family was awake and wailing at their sons' fate. Mary went in and spoke with the father.

"There's fever hereabouts," she said, "perhaps they've only swooned."

"Aw, you're daft, Mary Calhoun," said the father of the boys. "I know *dead* when I see it!"

Still and all, he let Mary go to the kitchen, where she got a bowl of water and her kerchief, as if to mop the boys' fevered brows. Upstairs, she fed them the oatmeal.

With the first morsel each boy stirred. With the second bite, each boy blinked and awoke. And with the third bite, each boy sat up and yawned or stretched, and said, "What terrible nightmares I've had."

Mary Calhoun lived a long and comfortable life. She came into some money later on, after she saved for years and bought the fallow land beside the graveyard. But throughout her life, no matter who died, rich or poor, great or small, her friend or not, she never went to the burial.

In fact, she never, ever went into that graveyard again.

THE MO MO

NOW, UP IN THE WOODS OF SOUTH NEW JERSEY, along the coast there, where the locals are called "pineys," they've got the New Jersey devil. Down south, you've got your skunk-ape. But there's not a monster around that can match up to what us hillbillies have seen ... the dreaded Mo Mo.

Now, Mo Mos get big. One feller up at Galena, almost up to Crane, was over in the national forest west of Cape Fair, and came around a corner in a Jeep, and his headlights hit something in the road right in front of him. It was Mo Mo! He can't describe him very well, though, except that he's big and black and hairy. if you ask about the critter's head, the feller just says, "I don't know. The headlights only reached up to its waist!!"

They've been seen all over. In the late '60s they were spotted in the wooded suburbs southwest of St. Louis, along the river, even over to Cape Girardeau, although I can't imagine why anyone, even a Mo Mo, would want to go there.

But the meanest, scariest Mo Mo was sighted around Mount Vernon about 1959. The feller that saw it told me he was coming back to the house from the fields just at dusk, and saw what he thought was an old farmer sitting in the unfenced field beside the road. As he got closer, he saw it was too big and too hairy to be a human being. It seemed to be sitting on its haunches, with its head resting on its hands, then it stood up abruptly!

It was about nine feet tall, and it strode across the road in front of the feller! It had long black hair all over it, and it had glowing orange eyes! When he got home, a lot of his chickens had been taken, and eaten in the field!

That's what Mo Mos do, they steal chickens. And they eat hogs. And they gut dogs, too. But they don't seem to eat the dogs.

So, I guess they have some sense after all.

SMOKEY JOE

ON THE BANKS OF THE BUFFALO RIVER IN ARKANSAS, there is a Boy Scout camp. At that camp, some boys hear tell a mighty strange story, and folks swear it's true!

Years ago some boys were away from their tents, playing in the riverbed. They got to splashing each other, then throwing handfuls of mud, then someone got angry, and the mud started to include rocks. Just as a Scoutmaster came along to break up the fight, the largest rock of all struck him hard in the side of the head!

The man went down hard, face down, in the riverbed. The boys were too scared to do anything, and ran for help. When they returned, he was gone! The man did not return to camp that season, in spite of extensive searches for him. At last the camp was closed up for the winter.

The next spring, with a new crop of Boy Scouts coming in, strange things happened. The doors to a food storage room were broken, as if by great strength. Things—primarily food items—disappeared from tent sites. Footprints were found, shadowy shapes were seen at night, and a mysterious lone silhouette was observed, high on the bluff across the cold, dark river, at the solitary tree known as antenna pine.

One day, a boy was out hiking alone, against camp rules, and began to climb the bluffs. He lost his footing, and fell from one ledge to a ledge below. He was knocked unconscious and suffered a broken ankle.

When he regained consciousness, he was no longer on the ledge!

He found himself alone in a bluff shelter, high up the cliff face over the river. His ankle was wrapped expertly with an old Ace bandage. The shelter was littered with cattle bones and food remains, and the area stank terribly. He climbed out as quickly as he could, and went down the cliff, hand over hand, to the camp.

In his haste and fear, he forgot the way back to the cave, and when questioned back at camp, was unable to tell exactly where he'd been. But his description of the smoked walls of the cave, and the smell, and the food leavings meant just one thing to the boys in the camp.

The boy had been rescued, thanks to the still-surviving instincts of the mysterious missing Scoutmaster that the kids at camp call ... Smokey Joe.

---

* In the jump variant of this story, when the old hillbilly asks "Wh-wh-at do you want here?" the storyteller jumps up from his or her rocking chair, grabs the nearest unsuspecting listener, and screamed: "I'm her after *you!*"

THE OLD BLACK BOOGER—I

THERE WAS THIS OLD MAN who swore up and down in blue streaks, fished on Sunday, never went to the church house, and cheated his neighbors when he could. He was so ornery that the preacher used him as the subject of one of his sermons! That's ornery!

"Someday," said the preacher, spittin' damnation and spoutin' hellfire, "that ol' black booger himself will come and get that man!" That was just another way of sayin' "the Devil," without actually saying his name right out.

Not long after that, one Sunday night, late, after everyone else had been to the church house but the ornery man, that man was sittin' all alone in his cabin in front of the fire. All of a sudden, the fire gave a *crack!* The old man sat up, havin' been about half asleep. Then there was a noise up the flue, and somethin' fell down the rock chimney into the fire. Sparks scattered all around.

Down the chimney came two big, black feet. They fell into the fire and fell out onto the hearth, like they'd been just cut off of something huge and horrible. The feet walked toward each other and stood side by side.

Down the chimney fell two long, skeleton-like legs, with big, black, knobby knees. The legs fell in the fire, then they got up and walked over and sat on the feet and stood side by side.

Down the chimney came crashing a big, muscular smoke-blackened body without any arms. It fell in the fire and rolled out onto the hearth, and got up. The legs kneeled down and took up the body, and it stood there, waiting.

By now the old man was tremblin' and sweatin'. Down the chimney rattled two huge arms with hands. They crawled by their fingers out of the fire and climbed up the swaying body. The old man was shakin' and starting to moan.

With a crash and explosion of sparks, something huge crashed into the fire. The body turned, and, with its new arms, lifted out of the fire a huge head with horns like a bull and fangs like a panther. The hands lifted the head into place, and the thing turned to face the old man. Two eyes that burned like hot coals opened up and stared at the man.

The old man was just about scared pretty near to death by now, but he asked, "W-w-what makes your feet so big?"

The thing answered in a deep voice, "From walking up and down the ends of this earth."

"W-w-what makes your shins so skinny and lithe?"

"From death and decay, starvation and dearth."

"W-w-w-what makes your shoulders and arms so wide?"

"From carrying wood and stoking the fires."

"W-w-what makes your head so huge?"

"From planning and plotting and evil desires."

The old man stood, tremblin', and started to back away.

"W-w-what name do you go by?" asked the old man.

The old black booger grinned like a wolf and worked his fingers in the air. "I am the Devil, collecting my due."

"Wh-wh-at do you want here?"

"All down the chimney, I've come after *you!*"

The old man let out a scream, and people two hollers away heard him screamin' for quite a while after that, before the cries echoed and faded and he was never heard from again.*

---

* In the jump variant of this story, when the old hillbilly asks "Wh-wh-at do you want here?" the storyteller jumps up from his or her rocking chair, grabs the nearest unsuspecting listener, and screamed: "I'm her after *you!*"

THE OLD BLACK BOOGER—II

This folk song is a completely different narrative, but is known by the insulting epithet in the name. The booger is blackhearted, not black in color, and is a foreign soldier (originally a British soldier) being boarded unwelcome. Some variants end with a ghoul reference, others do not.

Oh, yonder comes that old black booger.
Oh, I won't have him coming acrost the sea to marry me,
With his old shoe-boots and leggins.

My mother, she told me to open the door.
Oh, I won't have him! I opened the door and he fell on the floor,
With his old shoe-boots and leggins.

My mother, she told me to set him a chair.
Oh, I won't have him! I set him a chair and he looked like a deer,
With his old shoe-boots and leggins.

My mother, she told me to set him a plate.
Oh, I won't have him! I set him a plate and he et like a snake,
With his old shoe-boots and leggins.

My mother, she told me to fix him a bed.
Oh, I won't have him! I fixed him his bed and he stood on his head,
With his old shoe-boots and leggins.

My mother, she told me to bid him farewell.
So, I won't have him! I bade him farewell ... saw him rotting in hell,
With his old shoe-boots and leggins.

THE "MAY NEVER ARRIVE"

THE MISSOURI AND NORTH ARKANSAS RAILROAD'S engines bore the initials M&NA, but the folks in Boone County, Arkansas, got to calling it the "May Never Arrive." Scheduling and freight handling were not as precise on the M&NA as passengers might have desired. My grandfather lost his luggage on that train, and it turned up at a garage sale in Springfield, Missouri, ninety miles away and thirty years later (much to the delight of the Boone County Historical Museum, which now proudly displays the contents, the Masonic regalia of one of Harrison's most prominent citizens, Dr. Leonidas Kirby.)

After the railroad closed down, though, some vagrants along the tracks reported seeing, late at night, an unlit caboose, rolling silently along the tracks without a train. Some said it was the caboose from the train load of telephone-pole logs that derailed at high speed years before.

Others just said it was the ghost of the train itself, late to its own funeral.

The good old "May Never Arrive."

THE BOOGER UNDER NOB HILL

THERE ARE TWO NOB HILLS in the Ozarks of northwest Arkansas. One is the hill on which Artists' Point sits, on the deadliest curve on U.S. 71 between Fayetteville and Fort Smith. In the 1960s, my family lived on that property. The other Nob Hill is a small community east of Springdale, and in the early 1960s, there were some peculiar sightings there.

Somewhere under Nob Hill, along War Eagle Creek, a wanted criminal hid out for years; after he was captured, and spent years in an asylum, he told doctors and reporters that he had seen a hairy man in the creek valley.

Now, the hairy man has been seen all across the Southeast, all the way to East Texas, and may be the Fouke Monster of southwest Arkansas, too. But this was the only time I ever heard of a hairy man in the Arkansas Ozarks.

This hairy man was an albino, with red eyes, and long white hair, according to the dying man's delirious statements. It would have ended there, except for several sightings that came later, in or near the Nob Hill community.

After the 1970s, no one saw or spoke of the booger again, but every once in a while another story surfaces of someone who saw the hairy, albino man, the Booger under Nob Hill.

THE CREATURE IN THE HOLE

DOWN ALONG THE BUFFALO RIVER in the Arkansas Ozarks, three teenaged boys were going swimming and deep diving. They went down to the river near the mouth of Hemmed-In Hollow. There's a sharp bend in the river there, with a water-worn hole that's very deep. Even on the brightest days, the water looks black in that hole.

As they were swimming, they decided to dive down and see if there was a cave within the deep depression. It was late afternoon, and the sun was behind the bluffs. The hot sun and cold water had made wisps of fog in the cool coves. They were prepping for the dive, putting on their snorkels and fins, when an old woman walked out of the nearby woods, seemingly from out of nowhere.

She wore a very long skirt and a blouse and vest; she looked almost like a Gypsy woman. She approached them and asked if they were about to go swimming. They said, "Yes."

"Haven't you heard," she asked, "about the Creature in the Hole?"

They answered that they had not.

"The stories have it that there is a creature that lives down there in that hole," she said. "Some say it's half man, half fish!"

The boys said that was a crazy idea.

"No," she answered, "investigate it yourselves. A few

years ago a diver went down to see for himself, and barely escaped with his life." She turned and left while the boys were talking, and since they did not see her go, it seemed she had vanished.

After much discussion, they decided it was too late to dive that afternoon. No one would say he was scared, though.

The story could have ended there, except that several years later, some of the same young men took lessons in scuba diving from a prominent scuba diving school in southern Missouri. After the end of the lessons, there was a big party for all the students that had been enrolled.

As they sat around eating doughnuts and drinking soft drinks, the tale of the Creature in the Hole came up. The instructor said,

"That's an amazing coincidence! A diver I know from Springfield went scuba diving in a deep hole in the Buffalo River a few years back, and was attacked by what he described as a giant catfish! He just barely escaped with his life, and has scars on his leg to prove it!"

OLD WALLEYES

IN THE DEEP, DARK COVES of the river drainage lives Old Walleyes. (Now, a cove in the Ozarks ain't water, it's high, dry land: a narrow valley with steep cliff walls and often a cave or a falls at the head.) In one cove, in a deep limestone cave, Old Walleyes makes his home. He's a huge thing with four short legs and paws with long claws on the toes. His head is as big as a wagon and his mouth is as wide as a washtub. He'll eat man or beast or anything in between, and his teeth are as big as axe blades and twice as sharp.

The ghostliest part of him's his eyes, huge, vacant, cloudy things that see without seeing and stare you dead without looking. He may be blind, it's hard to say, but he can run like the devil wind on your trail when he's hungry for your flesh.

A man went to the slaughter house with his cow in tow behind his wagon, and had her butchered for beef on shares, with the butcher taking his payment in meat. The meat was loaded into his wagon and he started back home where the smokehouse was ready to hang the meat in. It was a cold day, so the meat would keep fine, but the man hurried to reach the homestead before dark. He took the shortcut past the cove, knowing he had plenty of time to get past Old Walleyes' den before darkness come .

On the twisting, hard shelf-rock road, a linchpin gave way,

and he lost a wheel offen the wagon. He worked frantically in the gathering darkness to bend a new linchpin out of hog wire to get the wheel back on before Old Walleyes' feeding time. The sun was racing behind the hill unnaturally fast, and the shadows were getting longer and longer. The man thought about abandoning the wagon, unhitching the horse, and riding on without his beef as the shadows got deeper and he struggled with the wheel. He thought about just lighting out and running, then it was too late and too dark even for that.

His only hope was to get the wagon wheel on and drive out fast.

The sounds came out from deep in the cave behind him as he worked: deep, horrible, hungry sounds! The horse began to stamp and shy and whinny.

Old Walleyes was coming out!

The man got the wheel onto the axle. He got the doubled-over hog wire through the pinhole. He bent the wire down, and jumped onto the wagon seat. As he flipped the reins, the horse bolted forward just as Old Walleyes put one huge claw onto the tailgate of the wagon!

The wooden tailgate splintered into a hundred pieces, but the horse pulled free and the wagon was bouncing along the hard road as fast as the terrified horse could run. The road cut between some close trees, and the Old Walleyes would just push 'em aside and push 'em over with his huge front feet. The wagon bounced over rocks and crashed along through brush alongside of the road. And Old Walleyes tore the dirt with his paws and scrabbled over the bedrock places with sparks flying offen his claws.

The beef bounced all around in the bed of the wagon, and the poor man bounced all around over the wagon seat.

Just as Old Walleyes opened his enormous mouth to take

the end offen the wagon, a slab of that beef bounced out onto the road. Old Walleyes stopped and sniffed the slab, then downed a hundred pounds of meat with one bloody gulp.

The man and the horse got thirty yards ahead in the time it took old Walleyes to eat the beef slab, but here he come again, breaking through the timber, catching up to the wagon. His hot, rotten breath blew over the man as he got closer and closer, and the man turned and kicked another slab of beef out onto the road. Old Walleyes stopped and sniffed the meat and tore it apart rib from rib and swallowed it with a horrible crunch!

The man thought he could hear his own ribs being crushed in that awful noise, and he screamed and drove the horse even faster than before. Old Walleyes was right up onto the wagon again, and the man kicked out the entire half a beef that was left.

Old Walleyes stopped, and sniffed, and et it down!

Just then the wagon reached the ford over the creek and the man ran the wagon over the ford at breakneck speed, throwing a plume of water fifteen feet high into the air. On the far side of the creek he turned the horse acrosst an open field and headed for his house.

Old Walleyes skidded to a stop at the edge of the creek, his claws cutting grooves in the bedrock. He stood there, with his cloudy eyes staring, beef blood pouring outten his mouth, sniffing the air for the horse and the man.

Old Walleyes can't climb trees, and he can't cross running water.

The man and his horse got home, but the wagon was never the same again.

JACK AND THE SALLY-BALLY

ONCE UPON A TIME in the wooded hills of the Ozarks, there lived a smart young boy named Jack. He had climbed a bean plant, and he had killed a giant, but now he was visiting his grandma and grandpa in their log cabin in a valley.

Up in the hills above Jack's grandma's cabin there lived a monster that folks called the Sally-Bally. He would come sallying forth into the valley and scare the people. He would eat their horses and cows and kick down their log cabins just to be mean. The Sally-Bally was one bad critter. Sometimes he even ate people!

It was autumn when Jack came for his visit. Jack's grandpa had a crop of apples in his orchard that were the biggest, reddest, sweetest apples Jack had ever seen. The smell of those apples cooking in a big black pot over an outdoor fire filled the valley.

All the neighbors smelled the apples when they were cooking.

So did the Sally-Bally.

That old Sally-Bally came down out of the hills, picked up the big black pot hot from the fire, and drank the apples like a jug of cider. He would have eaten Jack's grandma and grandpa too if they hadn't run away and hid' for two days.

Jack's grandpa needed to pick more apples to take to town

and sell for some cash money. Jack agreed to help him. They took two big buckets and went into the orchard to pick. The apples were so good that they ate a few while they were picking. The smell of those sweet, sweet apples filled the air and woke the sleeping Sally-Bally in his cave.

"You know," said Grandpa, "we ought to make a Sally-Bally trap and use these apples as bait." Soon they were both bragging about how easily they could catch that old Sally-Bally. They began to laugh and joke about it and forgot to keep watch for the Sally-Bally.

Sure enough, over the hill came the Sally-Bally, lured by the smell of the apples. The Sally-Bally was twenty feet tall, with eighteen feet of him legs. He had long, ugly hair and ears as big as the bed of a wagon. His arms hung so low they dragged the ground, and his mouth had so many teeth it looked like a laundry basket full of butcher knives!

The Sally-Bally roared like a mountain lion arguing with a steam engine. Jack and his grandpa began to run toward the house with the Sally-Bally chasing them. Jack threw down his bucket of apples, and the critter stopped to eat them—bucket and all. When the Sally-Bally had almost caught up to Jack and his grandpa, Grandpa threw down his bucket, and the critter stopped to eat those apples, too.

While the Sally-Bally was picking his teeth with the bail of the second bucket, Jack and Grandpa ran to the cabin and yelled for Grandma to run and hide.

"Run, Grandma," yelled Jack. "Here comes the Sally-Bally!"

Knowing they didn't have enough time to run away, Jack and Grandpa turned over the big black pot in the front yard and hid under it.

Grandma was sitting on the front porch taking in the cool

breeze and weaving on her wooden loom. She saw Jack and his grandpa come running. She even saw the Sally-Bally come over the hill and look around for them after they had hidden under the big black pot. But Grandma was a tough old lady, and she just puffed on her pipe and went on weaving on her loom.

The Sally-Bally came dragging over to the cabin, stepped over the black pot without looking under it, and growled at Grandma. "Where are those menfolks at?" growled the Sally-Bally.

"I ain't seen them," said Grandma weaving on her loom.

"You'd better tell me where they're at," said the Sally-Bally, leaning over the roof of the porch and blowing his hot stinky breath down on Grandma, "or I'll smash your porch flat!"

The porch was Grandma's most favorite place to be, so that threat made her mad. "Lean over here close if you want to hear," she said to the Sally-Bally. He leaned way down and put his big old ear to the porch.

Quick like a bunny rabbit Grandma jumped into the Sally-Bally's hairy old ear and pulled her loom and rocking chair in after her. Then she sat back down and went back to work, rocking in her chair and weaving on her loom. The noise almost drove the Sally-Bally crazy!

The rocking chair squeaked and the weaving loom creaked. The Sally-Bally jumped around in circles, hollering and yelling. He scratched his ear and he shook his head and he rolled on the ground. But Grandma was used to riding in a wagon over the roads in the Ozarks, and this ride in the critter's ear was mild by comparison.

Finally the Sally-Bally couldn't stand the noise of the rocking chair and the weaving loom any longer. He decided to beat his head against a nearby cliff to see if he couldn't knock the grandma and her furniture out of his ear. He stood beside the cliff and beat his big ugly head on the rock so hard that he fell down dead.

By now Jack and his grandpa had come out from under the black pot and had run up to help Grandma. They carried the loom between them and Grandma carried the rocking chair upside down on her head. The three walked back to the cabin in the valley and cooked a big pot of apples.

"Well," said Jack to his grandma, "now that you've killed the Sally-Bally what are you going to do with him?"

"Ain't going to do nothing," said Grandma. "The moss will grow on him, and the ferns will grow on him, and the weeds will grow on him, and by next spring you won't even know he was ever there."

And, you know, she was right!

THE GOWEROW IN MARVEL CAVE

THERE'S A CAVE IN EASTERN STONE COUNTY in Missouri, above Indian Arrowpoint, called Marble Cave (now known as Marvel Cave). A boy, out for a walk gathering ginseng, passed the deep mouth of that cave, which drops straight down into nothing. He sat at the edge for a while, enjoying the cool air that comes up out of the cave at that time of the day.

While he was a-sitting there, he heard the most awfullest noise come up out of the cave. It sounded like thunder and a panther and an angry bull and the noise a mule's hoof makes when it comes out of deep mud. The feller jumped up and nearly fell in, he was so startled. After he listened a long while, he decided to see what he could see in that old cave.

Back at the cabin, he got a candle lantern, a long rope and a flatiron off the hearth. He went back to the cave and tied the flatiron onto the bottom of the rope to keep it from swinging too much, like a plumb bob. Then he struck a light and lit the lantern, and tied it up the rope about eight feet, so when the iron hit the cave floor, the light would be up fairly high still.

He stood very carefully at the edge, with his feet planted on rock, and lowered the flatiron into the cave mouth. Down went the lantern into the darkness after the iron.

As he was lowering the lantern, he saw the dull glow of two huge eyes looking up at him, reflecting the lantern light.

There was a deep growly snort of some kind, and the lantern blew out. The rope jiggled around a bit, like something had bumped against it. The old boy pulled the rope up as fast as he could. The lantern was fine.

But something had bit' the flatiron half in two.

THE BOOGER DOG

A BOOGER DOG, huge, black, and ghostly, has been seen in Taney and Stone Counties in Missouri for nearly a century. The booger dog is bigger than a boar, almost as big as a bull, and leaves huge footprints in the snow that farmers find crossing their fields. Night hunters have seen the thing and missing cattle have been blamed on it. Some folks say it is the familiar spirit in the service of a family of witch women, handed down from witch mother to witch daughter. Others say it is a witchman who can change into that form to go out and do devilment.

But those who've lived around here longest say it's a ghost of an infidel who lived in Taney County.

Now, an infidel is someone who hates the church house and won't help raise the building when the whole neighborhood's getting together for a church raising. He won't come to brush arbor meetings, and he won't let anybody say grace over their food if they eat at his cabin.

Everybody dies sooner or later, and as this infidel was dying, he was cursing and as faithless as ever. Some of the neighbors came over to sit with him, and at least one pious farmer began to carry on about hellfire and damnation in the hopes of getting a deathbed conversion for the ornery cuss. In the midst of all the talk, the cabin roof caught fire. Some say it was lightning, others say sparks from the fireplace set a flue fire in the creosote soot in the chimney.

As the house was burning, the neighbor men tried to get the old infidel out of bed, but even though there were three of them, they couldn't lift him. All of a sudden he weighed as much as a bull. The men tried to move the bed, but it wouldn't budge. Something was holding the old infidel in his place.

About that time the burning roof came down around them, and the neighbors ran out the door, giving the old man up for lost. As they ran out, a large black dog ran out under their feet. They figured that it must have been under the bed.

After the logs burned down, and the chimney fell in, the farmers sifted through the ashes looking for the bones of the infidel to bury on his own property.

There weren't any bones in the ash!

And a booger dog, bigger than life and blacker than night, has been seen ever since.

THE BOOGER CATS

ONE YOUNG SPORT WAS WALKING from the county seat back to his home in the hills; it was a two-day walk. On the way home, he stopped at a deserted cabin to spend the night. The place was ramshackled, and the log walls were going catywhompus, but the chimney was sound, so the young sport struck a fire. He was sitting by the hearth when a stray black cat came in the front door and sat near him. He looked at the cat, and the cat looked at him and licked its chops.

A few minutes later, a larger black cat came sauntering in and sat by the first. The sport looked at the cats, and the cats looked at him and licked their chops.

The bigger cat looked at the smaller one and said, "Shall we start?"

"No," said the smaller cat. "Let's wait for Martin."

The sport was a little scared, but he didn't say anything, just stared into the fire.

A few minutes later, the largest black cat the sport had ever seen came wandering in the door and sat by the other two. The sport looked at the cats, and the cats looked back at him and licked their chops.

The biggest cat looked at the other two and said, "Shall we start?"

"No," said the littlest cat, "Let's wait for Martin."

The young sport was starting to shiver, but he didn't say anything, just stared into the fire.

A few minutes later, another cat came sashaying in through the empty door frame. This cat was as large as a young bull, must've weighed three hundred pounds. It sat down by the other cats and curled its five-foot-long tail around its huge feet. The young man looked over at the cats, and the cats looked back at him and licked their chops. The huge one's teeth were as long as a man's fingers, and sharp as butcher knives.

The huge cat looked at the others and said in a deep, growling voice, "Shall we start?"

"No," said the kitten in its little-bitty voice. "Let's wait for Martin."

The young sport jumped up and ran out of the cabin as fast as he could. As he disappeared down the dirt road, the cats could hear him holler, "Tell Martin I couldn't wait!"

THE CAT'S PAW

FOLKS SAY THAT WHAT I AM ABOUT TO TELL YOU happened over in Indian Territory, but the fact is it happened right here in Missouri. After hog-scalding one autumn, one feller let his smokehouse air out and packed it with all his smoked pork. In those days no one thought of putting a lock on a smokehouse door; a latch was enough to keep the hounds out.

Soon, some of this feller's meat was missing. Now, iffen a neighbor needed some meat, he wouldn't've come and stole' it. He'd've come up and asked for the loan of it, with a promise to pay back as soon as possible. So the feller knew there was something else going on.

He hid out in the smokehouse with his shotgun. He had a cleaver hung on the wall of the smokehouse to cut off meat with, so he took it down and hung onto it, just in case the thief got any ideas.

After an hour or two of darkness, by moonlight, the latch on the smokehouse door rattled free and fell against the door. The feller inside stiffened awake and sat almost without breathing. The door opened slowly, and a huge panther stepped in, walking on its hind feet. It looked around, like it smelled the feller hiding in the dark corner, but all it could smell was the meat. The panther reached for a ham.

The feller stepped out of the darkness and swung the heavy cleaver. He cut the forepaw off the cat, who spun and flipped and ran out howling. The man grabbed the bloody paw off the ham, before the blood could sour the meat, and ran inside his house. He barred the door to keep the cat out, and threw the paw under his bed to make a good luck charm from the next day.

Most of the night the great cat could be heard howling and complaining, and there were heavy footfalls on the porch from time to time, but by dawn all was quiet.

After dawn, a neighbor came over and said his wife had been up before dawn to chop some wood and had cut her hand off. She had bled to death, the man said, and could this feller's wife come over and help with the laying out of the body. The lady of the house put on her shawl and went with the neighbor.

After she left, the feller went to his bed to get the panther's paw and make a good luck charm. He reached under the bed, but couldn't feel the paw anywhere. He got down on all fours and looked under the bed.

There on the floor was a woman's hand in a pool of blood.

Now, a witch is supposed to be able to change into any form she wants, and change back at dawn. But you don't believe that, do you? The feller didn't either, but he fed the hand to the hogs and never told anybody about it but me.

THE CAT KING

THERE ARE SOME MIGHTY STRANGE THINGS that happen right around Halloween, and folks don't try to explain 'em.

One Halloween, along before dark, a feller was walking down the path and came to an abandoned cabin. There were dozens of cats running around the cabin, fat cats, skinny cats, old cats, young cats, white cats and black cats. Lots of black cats. The feller stopped and stood, kind of spellbound, and stared at all those cats.

Finally, one of those cats turned and stared back at the feller, and after a moment or two, the cat spoke up and said:

"When you get to the next house, tell that old striped cat that Old Kitty Rollins is dead."

Then the cat ran on into the cabin, and the man, terrified, lit out and ran on down the path.

After about a mile or so the feller had slowed down to a walk, and came across an old closed-up house. On the front porch sat an old, striped cat, twitching its tail. The feller walked over to the fence, and leaned over. He looked straight at the old cat and said, "The cat down the lane said to tell you 'Old Kitty Rollins is dead.' "

Straight-way the old cat jumped up and dashed down the path the way the feller had come. As he passed the cat yelled:

"I'll be king yet!"

III. A TWIST O' THE TALE

The twist in the endings of these ghost and ghoul tales
makes them favorites at ghost storytelling parties,
even if the listeners have heard them all before.

SHE'S GOT ME!

ONCE, NOT LONG AGO, in the farmland in the North, there was a community of plain folks who used the old-style farm tools instead of modern tractors and things. The menfolk were out in the field working one day, and two young girls had taken supper out to their fathers and uncles and brothers in the field. Walking home with nothing left of the meal except the dirty forks in their apron pockets, the girls passed the old iron gate of the graveyard.

"There's where they buried that old witch today," said the sassy girl to the polite girl just as the sun was going down.

"Oh, you must not speak ill of the dead," said the polite girl. "That isn't nice at all!"

"I'm not afraid of that old woman," said the brazen girl. "You're just a fraidy-cat. Why, I'd go in and just spit on that old woman's grave. But you'd be too scared to come with me!"

"Even if she were a witch," said the polite girl, "it would be wrong of you to do that. Besides, you'd just go in there and wait behind a tree. Then you'd come out and claim you'd done it!"

"I would not," the other answered. "I'll just go right in and spit on that old witch's grave. And to prove I did it ..." she pulled a fork out of her apron pocket as she spoke. "I'll stick this fork into the grave to prove I was there. You can go in tomorrow in broad daylight and see."

With the fork in her hand, the sassy girl went through the old iron gate into the dark graveyard and walked among the trees and tombstones until she came to the fresh grave of the old woman. The sun was down, and long shadows fell across the pile of dirt that covered the grave. It was hard to see in the darkness, but the brazen girl leaned over and spit on the dirt.

"Take that, old witch," said the girl, and she bent over and stuck the fork into the dirt to show she had been there. Just then, she felt something grab onto the hem of her long dress. When she tried to stand up, it pulled at her dress. She looked down in the darkness and saw something white, like the bones of a hand holding onto her, pulling her back down. She screamed, "She's got me!" and fainted.

Outside the graveyard, the polite girl heard the scream and ran back to the field to get her father and brothers. The men were already walking home for the night and met her on the road. She told them what had happened, and they hurried to the graveyard with one candle lantern to light their way. Inside the graveyard, the polite girl led the men and boys all the way back through the trees to the grave of the old woman. There lay the body of the sassy girl, fallen over the grave. When the men lifted the girl she woke up.

Everyone laughed. When the sassy girl had bent over and stuck the fork in the ground, she had caught the bottom of her own dress. It was only the fork that had grabbed her and held her to the old witch's grave.

WHO'S FOLLOWING ME?

ONE DARK NIGHT, a little boy had stayed in the park too long. It was late, and his mother was going to be mad. It was dark, and it was a long, long way to his house. He started walking slowly out of the park.

He walked slowly along. Each time he took a step, he heard something behind him take a step, walking slowly along. He stopped and looked back. There was no one there. "Who's following me?" he said.

He walked a little faster. Each time he heard his shoe hit the sidewalk, he heard something else make a sound, like someone behind him taking a step—walking a little faster. He stopped and looked back. There was no one there. "Who's following me?" he said.

He started to run just a little. Each time his foot hit the ground, he heard something else, like feet behind him hitting the ground—starting to run just a little. He stopped and looked back. There was no one there ... that he could see.

He started to run fast. Each stride he took, he heard someone behind him taking a stride—starting to run fast. He didn't stop. He didn't look back. He ran and he ran and he ran.

He ran to his block and he ran to his yard and he ran to his porch. On the porch he stopped and looked back. There was no one there. But when he took another step he heard that noise again. He looked down at his shoe.

The sole was coming off his old shoe, and every time he took a step, the loose sole flapped and made a noise. He had been running from himself!

RED VELVET RIBBON

LONG AGO AND FAR AWAY lived a fancy rich man with a big black silk hat and a fine silk tie. He went out walking every day, hoping some pretty girl would see him and fall in love with him and become his bride.

He met a lot of ladies in the park, but he was just a little too snooty for them. They didn't like him very much.

He met a lot of ladies down by the riverside where people go rowing in boats, but he bragged just a little too much for them. They didn't like him very much.

He even tried visiting the graveyard. There he met a pretty lady in a pretty white dress with a red velvet ribbon tied around her neck. He admired the red velvet ribbon, and as they talked, he reached up and touched it.

"That's my red velvet ribbon," she said, "and you can't ever take it off."

Time passed. Spring became summer, summer became autumn. The rich man with the big black silk hat and the fine silk tie fell in love with the pretty lady in the pretty white dress with the red velvet ribbon tied around her neck.

At their wedding, he wore his big black silk hat and his fine silk tie, and she wore a lovely wedding dress—and her red velvet ribbon around her neck.

On their honeymoon, he touched her lovely neck and

touched the red velvet ribbon, but she said, "You can't ever take it off."

The next year they had a baby. They were both very happy, but the fancy rich man was beginning to be bothered by that red velvet ribbon. He could buy anything he wanted. He could afford anything he wanted. But he couldn't take that red velvet ribbon off his wife's neck.

Finally, when the baby was one year old, the fancy rich man couldn't stand it any longer. While his pretty wife was taking a nap and the baby was sound asleep in her crib, he crept into the room and sneaked up on his sleeping wife.

Very gently, he untied the red velvet ribbon.

Very gently, he removed the red velvet ribbon.

Very gently, her head rolled to the side, rolled off the bed, and fell to the floor!

THE HEADLESS FOREIGNER

THEY SAY THERE WAS AN OLD MAN and an old woman that lived up at Forsyth, Missouri, who kept all their money, saved for years, in an iron lockbox. The old man was a dead shot with his pistol, which he carried in his belt all the time, so the couple wasn't scared of anybody or anything.

One night they were cooking supper and there came two young men with funny accents into the house yard, and hollered at the old man. He went out on the porch with his pistol in his hand, and the two young fellows asked if they could buy supper at his place. Since the old man never turned down a chance to make another silver dime, he invited them in.

The old woman cooked up extra greens and things and served them out on the table for the four of them. The young men talked friendly-like, and sometimes they'd say something to one another in a foreign tongue, which sounded to the old man like Gypsy talk. Soon, the two young men were talking in a low voice kind of monotonously, sort of to no one in particular, and the old folks found they were getting kind of sleepy. Then the two started to argue in their heathen talk, but that didn't bother the old folks, who kept on eating. Finally, one of the foreign fellows stood up and said, "We are quarreling in your house. Please excuse us; we will go outside and settle this."

The two went outside, and the old folks followed along.

The tall one suddenly whipped a knife out of his belt, and cut the other man's throat. The shorter one stood for a moment, weaving back and forth, and the tall one swung the knife again and took the other's head clean off. As the tall one ran back into the house, the two old people stood on the porch and watched the headless body sway slightly and then fall to the ground. The bloody head flew backward behind the body, and rolled to a stop against a tree.

The two old folks just stood there hypnotized.

The eyes in the bloody head opened, and it spoke.

"Come and pick me up," said the head.

The body got up slowly, like a drunken man, and turned toward the head.

"Over here," said the head, "by the rosebush."

The couple just stood there and watched as the body felt around and found the head, and picked it up, and put it back in its place. Then he tied a red bandana around his neck to hold his head in place and walked off down the road without saying a word.

The old folks stood there for a long while without saying anything, watching the foreigner disappear down the lane. The sun went down, and they went inside and lit the lamp.

The house was empty. The tall man wasn't in there, and the iron box was open. The key was in the lock, instead of where it had been hid in the sugar bowl on the mantelpiece.

The old man hitched up his team and took his wagon in town, but the sheriff just laughed at him. The old man's neighbors just shrugged, and said the old couple had been witched, like was done in olden times, by those Gypsies.

IV. LANTERNS OF THE LOST

The most haunting tales we hear and tell are
about those most palpable of spirits, the ghost lights.

HEADLESS BRAKEMAN

ON A DARK NIGHT, IN THE HEAT OF SUMMER, we left the sawmill where we worked and drove eighty miles to see it: the ghost light at Crossett, Arkansas. Four of us drove in a convertible with the top down—one of the guys had been there before and knew the way. It was about ten o'clock when we stopped on the gravel road and turned out the lights. The rail bed is elevated in that part of the state. The road rose about three feet above the level of the fields to cross the single set of rails.

We sat in the car drinking and talking, waiting for something to happen, daring and double-dog-daring each other to approach the light if it appeared. Somebody retold the legend in the steamy darkness:

A train had rolled to a stop just at this crossing sometime in the early 1900s, on a dark hot night like this one. A brakeman was walking the rail bed with a lantern, checking the cars or the couplings. Something, no one knew what, caught his attention between two cars; leaning in at the coupling he found something wrong.

Trying to fix something, a loose coupling or a dragging chain, he bent closer and closer to the metal mechanism. The locomotive lurched a few inches along the track as steam engines sometimes did, and a heavy ripple of movement surged down the long line of flatcars and boxcars. The brakeman's lantern fell to the rail bed.

Looking back past the coal car, the engineer saw the lantern fall. He took his own lantern and ran back, car after car, to where the brakeman's lantern lay. The brakeman's body was lying across the track. The head was lying under a bloody coupling. Some folks say the body went that night in a boxcar, but the head was left behind, no one having the courage to pick it up. Or maybe the head just wasn't in the boxcar with the body.

Anyway, by night people still see the light of the lantern, moving slowly along the tracks about three feet off the ground. "It's the decapitated brakeman," people say, "still looking for his head!"

The convertible got very quiet after the last retelling of the legend.

An instant later we saw it. A faint, yellowish ball of light about a foot in diameter was floating slowly along the tracks, three feet above the rails, coming north. It just crept along, not bobbing or weaving, just slow and steady.

Finally, on a double-dog-dare, I left the car and walked toward the tracks, not ever taking my eyes off the light, trying to meet it at the intersection. I was sweating, but I wasn't sure why. There wasn't any fear, or any feeling at all—just that light. I got onto the tracks and turned and faced it as it came slowly toward me. When it got within ten feet of me, it just vanished.

I was almost disappointed. After a minute, I turned to walk back to the car. There was the light, north of me on the tracks, moving away. The guys were all wide-eyed as I came up to the car.

"What did it feel like?" they asked.

"What did what feel like?" I said.

"We saw the ghost light pass right through your chest!"

Then, and only then, was I afraid. Really afraid.

THE SENATH LIGHT

IN THE BOOT HEEL OF MISSOURI, at the small town of Senath, there is a ghost light. We got some directions on how to get there: you turn off the pavement on County Road A at a certain point, drive a certain distance down a gravel road, cross a couple of bridges, then you're out in a soybean field and you come to a corner where there's an old, gnarled tree "with a lot of character."

We knew the tree the minute we saw it in the dusk light; it was a tree you might see in a horror film. You take another left, go down to another bridge, and park on the bridge. The hollow sounds echoing up from the old wooden bridge made the place pretty scary just to begin with. Real or imagined, the creaks and groans of the wooden bridge heightened our awareness as we waited for the light.

Then we saw the lights, far ahead of us. There are all the usual explanations: swamp gas, lights at some distant airport, but these lights didn't look anything like that. They drifted slowly toward us, fairly high up, yellow-white in color, moving about above the road and the fields. Five of us sat and watched them come closer and closer. Then the bridge noises and the slow approach of the lights combined to give us all the excitement we had been looking for that night.

We left. In reverse. Quickly.

THE MIAMI LIGHT

ON A DARK, FOGGY NIGHT one autumn, just outside of Miami, Oklahoma, a woman sent her daughter out to look for the cows and drive them back to the lot. This was in the late nineteenth century, so the daughter took a lighted lantern with her to cut the fog. The girl never came back. Her mother became frightened and began to search for the girl about midnight. She also carried a lantern.

She searched all night and never found her daughter, but the cattle were scattered across the rolling hills. The mother continued to search, night after night, insane with grief. When she died of remorse, her spirit continued to walk on foggy nights in the fall. She can still be seen, or her lantern can, on cold, foggy nights. I have seen the light; it's yellow like a lantern, and it swings just a little bit as if the ghost were carrying it while walking.

THE HORNET LIGHT

IN 1886, SETTLERS about eleven miles southwest of Joplin, Missouri, began to see a ghostly light. It was blamed on the ghost of a Quapaw Indian (the Quapaw Agency was at Seneca a few miles away) looking for his lost lover, who had committed suicide rather than give in to her father's wish that she marry a man of his choosing instead of the young Quapaw. The light scared some settlers so badly that they abandoned their farms and moved away. Today, the light is called the Hornet Spook Light, named for the settlement a few miles away.

THE HORNET BURIAL GROUND

I USED TO KNOW AN OLD Cherokee man who ran a liquor store just outside of Seneca, Missouri, south of Joplin, about where Highways 71 and 66 cross. This Indian man told me that when the road was cut through the area, the construction disturbed an Indian burial ground near Hornet. Those spook lights you see started being seen about the time the graves were disturbed.

The lights are the spirits of those disturbed burials, wandering in search of their scattered parts.

THE SPLIT HORNET LIGHT

YEARS AGO, WHEN I WAS QUITE YOUNG, I had just gotten out on my own, and was working at a job in Joplin, Missouri. A young man that I had been seeing came to me one evening and said, "You've got to come see this."

He said he wanted me to see the spook light south of Joplin. I assumed that it must be ... an excuse, you know. We were sitting at the side of the road with the lights off, and as we were talking and cuddling, a very bright, white light came up behind the car. It was beautiful! It was glowing white with blue fringes. It came directly toward the trunk, and when it got to the car, it split in two, and slowly passed by us on either side of the car, up about as high as the windows. It made no sound at all!

When it reached the hood, it rejoined and went on down the road.

THE STILL HORNET LIGHT

WHEN I WAS IN HIGH SCHOOL, a whole bunch of my buddies and I decided, one night, girls and guys, to go up to Hornet, Missouri, to see the spook light. One of us knew the way, from up in our corner of Oklahoma, closest to Missouri, and wanted all of us to go up and check on it.

We saw the spook light do something it hardly ever does, just sit absolutely still. It was yellow, shaded toward orange. It was about the size of a basketball, and it was sitting in an open field about three feet off the ground.

Very quietly, from about two hundred feet out, we encircled the light, all the way around it. Some fools will tell you that what causes the spook light is headlights from the Will Rogers Turnpike in Oklahoma, but when I was in high school the Turnpike hadn't been built yet. And the light is seen in the hollows between the hills. There's not any way that the intelligence this light displays in its movement could come from headlights.

Very quietly, speaking to each other, we all took one step forward, then another, then another. The light was just hanging there, three feet off the ground. We all took one more step, and when we got about fifty feet from it, it winked out.

The light immediately appeared a hundred yards away, off to one side, just hanging in midair. At that point, a lot of us had run out of courage, so we left.

V. TRUTHFUL TALES

It seems that everyone in the Ozarks knows of at least one ghost personally, or knows someone who knows of one personally, or knows someone who knows someone who ...

THE BABY IN THE BACK ROOM

WHEN WE FIRST MOVED TO NEWTON COUNTY in the Arkansas Ozarks from California, the house we moved into was a remodeled log cabin. Where they had cut doors through the log walls you could see how large the logs were, and the huge handmade square nails that had been used.

When we first arrived, when I was at the cabin alone, I could often hear a baby crying. We did have pet cats, but that was not what I was hearing. The sound was at the back of the house—in a back room, or where a lean-to or an older, long since destroyed back room had once been.

We had trouble with our well, and sometimes I would have to go out and work with the pump to get water in the middle of the night. That was most often when I heard the crying sounds. I finally became very frightened of that land, that cabin, and especially the area around the well. But the cause of the crying wasn't the well; the well itself was not very old. I believe it was the back area of the house that was the site of the ghostly sounds.

Babies very often died in the nineteenth century, having been born at home and subject to infection, and sometimes a feud or renegade attack in the Civil War might kill all the members of a family except a baby sleeping in the back room, unknown to the attackers.

That has most often been suggested as the cause for the crying that I heard.

BABY IN THE CAVE

DURING THE CIVIL WAR, some of my relatives lived over in eastern Arkansas. There was a young woman and a baby, and two older boys. They were afraid of the Yankees coming through, so she took the boys and they came west to hide in a cave. The troops did come through, and the neighbors soon missed the woman and her family. They searched the area and eventually found the two boys, living in the woods, living on berries. The mother and the baby had somehow stayed in the cave until they starved.

Although the bodies were eventually brought out and buried at the old farm place, the people who lived near the cave claim that they can still hear the baby crying in the cave.

One of the two boys who survived grew up to be the grandfather of my cousin; he told me the story years ago.

THE GHOST AT BOBO

THE CIVIL WAR COMMUNITY OF BOBO was near Old Carrollton, the seat of Old Carroll County in Arkansas (before it was cut in two to form Carroll and Boone Counties). At Bobo there was a two-story house that was made into a hospital for Confederates after the battle at Elkhorn Tavern, which the Yankees called Pea Ridge.

Folks who live in the area say they still see wounded Confederates out walking at night every decade or so, heading to or from the hospital, refusing to believe that their lives bled out on that wooden floor nearly two centuries ago.

THE GHOST IN THE CHURCH

THERE ARE A FEW OLD BUILDINGS that weren't burned during the Civil War still standing near the Crooked Creek area of Boone County, Arkansas. A very few houses were spared, and so were church houses. One of those old churches was north of my house on a dirt road north of Bear Creek Springs on the way to the little community of Denver.

My date and I went parking there one autumn night, and we parked at the small cemetery beside the then disused church building that dated back to the war. While we were ... talking, my date looked over at the church and gasped.

We could see a face in the window, looking out of the church at us. It looked like a bearded and ragged Confederate soldier, but I suspected it was some of my neighbor kids playing a trick. I got the Coleman lantern out of the pickup bed and went into the church. There was nothing inside, and I looked out the window toward the car.

When I got back to the car to report that it must have just been a reflection in the moonlight, my date told me what she had seen.

When I looked out, the face vanished, but as soon as I was gone, it faded back into view. When I looked, it was still looking out at us, and it was grinning this time.

That was when we left!

THE GHOST OF FLOYD EDINGS

ONE OF THE STRANGEST STORIES told in the Ozarks is the ballad of Floyd Edings (sometimes spelled Eddings). Floyd was the son of "Doc" Edings, and got into trouble in the 1880s and was lodged in the old county jail at Old Carrollton. In the early 1800s, Carrollton had been the county seat of Carroll County, Arkansas, and for half a century, through the Civil War, it was a seat of justice. After Boone County was founded, carved from the eastern half of Carroll, the seat was moved west to Berryville, but the old jail was still sometimes used for local prisoners awaiting transport to Berryville.

The jail at Old Carrollton was a marvel, hailed as escape-proof. The walls were three logs thick, with the outer and inner layers of log being horizontal, and the internal layer being vertical. There was only one opening, an iron door that was locked with a heavy padlock on the outside. During daylight hours a jailer was in attendance outside the log building, but at night the prisoner was locked in and on his own. Only one person was usually kept in the 18-foot by 18-foot interior.

In the century that has passed, the details of the event have become blurred. Some folks say the cell was being heated with a wood stove and the stove caught the building on fire. Others say the prisoner set the fire, planning to burn his way out or escape when he was let out of the burning building. Still others say opponents in an interfamily feud ignited the jail for revenge against Old Doc.

What did happen that is known for sure is this:

Deep in the night the jailhouse was on fire, and before his screams for help could awaken the community and bring the jailer with the key, the log fortress was consumed in flame and Floyd Edings was burned alive. When the fire was extinguished and the door cooled enough to be opened, the charred corpse of the boy was brought out. Here the versions of the story differ.

Some say the boy had written on the floor of the jail the words to a ballad about himself. Others say the ballad was written on a piece of paper, clutched tightly in one charred hand, its edges burned away. Some say a balladeer wrote it after the fact. There is another explanation, but here are the lyrics to the mournful song, sung to two different tunes by different storytellers today. Since Floyd was barely literate, the spelling has been cleaned up.

> *"My name is Floyd Edings, I'm the son of Old 'Doc.'*
> *He newly did disown me but I am one of his flock.*
> *Hell is my portion, I go naked, without a cent.*
> *For into Old Carrollton a-robbing I went.*
> *I went into Green Forest and hurried to work.*
> *They come and handcuffed me and took me to court.*
> *They summoned a jury, never cost them one cent.*
> *And for a little 'courting' to Berryville I went.*
> *When court was over to Old Carrollton [I] returned,*
> *And there in the jailhouse to death I was burned.*
> *They brung me my supper and locked the door fast.*
> *And left me there, lonely, to think on my past.*
> *I sent for my father, I thought it all well.*

But he never come nigh me, and I wished him in Hell.
No father, no mother, no money to spend.
They left me here lonely, myself to defend.
The jailhouse caught fire, and I called out for he'p.
They never come nigh me, just lay there and slep'.
The plaguèd old jailer went after the key.
He never did find it 'til the jail fire burnt me.
I laid on the floor with my blanket wrapped 'roun'.
They never come nigh me 'til the jailhouse burned down!"

Whatever Floyd's crimes, for which he was disowned by his father, they were probably no more than a simple robbery. Certainly few people believe that criminals should be burned alive, and the public quickly caught on to the ballad and sang it sorrowfully about a ne'er-do-well who got worse than he deserved.

It seems very unlikely that a fire hot enough to char the body the way it is always described would not burn a piece of paper in the boy's hand. It seems very unlikely that he could write so calmly and eloquently on the floor of a burning jail. A balladeer could have composed the song from the viewpoint of the boy after his death has already occurred.

Or maybe, just maybe, it was the ghost of Floyd Edings who dictated the song to the balladeer.

THE GRINNING GHOST

WE WERE OUT CAMPING ONE DAY, up near Columbia, Missouri, on a hiking trail. We got to the campsite at the trailhead just before nightfall on the night of the full moon. We set camp, and the moon came out so bright that you didn't need a flashlight. We decided to go hiking along the trail for a ways before we bedded down for the night.

As we walked along, we passed an old house place, with an old log cabin. As we walked up on the lawn, I swear I heard children playing, but there was no one around. Just an old empty log cabin and a few fallen-down outbuildings. I walked into the cabin, and Patricia followed me.

We were looking around, and there wasn't much in the cabin but some broken-down wooden furniture or boxes. It was really great to be in this old place, and I thought to myself,

"If these walls could just talk, what a story they could tell."

Then I heard a voice saying, "Get out of here! I don't want you here!"

I turned immediately, from the force of the voice, and started walking back out the door.

Patricia said something like, "Where are you going?"

I said, "I'm getting out of here!"

She said, "But I like it here, this is nice."

And I said, "I don't know, you can stay if you want to.

I'm leaving." And I walked to the door.

She said, "What's the matter?"

And I said, "I was told to leave."

"But I was told to stay," she said. At that she looked back into the cabin, and saw something I didn't see, because I was leaving. It was a man in this empty log cabin. He was flirting with her, smiling and waving to her.

We both left, and went outside, and didn't look back in. It was later, as we were explaining what each of us had heard or seen, that we realized she'd seen a ghost, a grinning ghost. A ghost who wanted me to go, but wanted Patricia to stay!

THE GHOST PLAYS POOL

WE BOUGHT AND MOVED INTO A HOUSE that had been owned by a man who never married and died of cancer while lying in the living room under the bay window in about 1982. From the day we moved into the house, we had trouble keeping it warm. It was a perfectly nice house, but it had cold spots in it. And it would creak; I always thought it was the house settling after the heat of the day. We had put our pool table in the basement, the same room the old owner had used as his rec room, and one he spent a lot of time in, being single.

The kids had been down playing pool one night, and I didn't ever know if they would rack the balls for the next night before they came up, or what. But one night I woke up and heard a ball hit the bottom of a pocket, and roll down the return trough to the storage rack.

The table was a weighted one, and it was leveled properly, so the balls weren't rolling into the pockets from gravity or anything. I checked on the kids and everyone was in bed but me, and whoever was playing pool downstairs. This happened every once in a while, but I had never gone down to see what was happening in the middle of the night.

One night I decided to rack the balls and leave them for a game myself, and I watched to see that no one went downstairs after I'd done it. About 2:00 or 3:00 in the morning I awoke when I heard the balls break. I jumped out of bed and landed on my feet. My daughter and I, and a nephew staying with us, hit the hall at the same time. We all went to the head of the stairs to the basement, and listened to the balls dropping, one by one, like someone was playing, into the pockets, into the return trough and rolling down into the storage tray.

My daughter said, "Mom, go down there and see what it is."

Well, I didn't go.

I got up early the next morning and went down in the daylight. All the balls I had racked the night before were in the tray. One cue, which I had put in the rack on the wall, was lying catty-cornered across the end of the table.

From then on when we were through playing, we just left the balls on the tray. The old man had to find some other ghostly entertainment after that.

THE GHOST ON THE THIRD FLOOR

AT THE MUSIC BUILDING AT HARDING COLLEGE in Searcy, Arkansas, there is a tradition that a ghostly piano player practices by night. From the second floor of the music building, you can hear a piano being played on the floor above you.

According to the story, a young man and a young woman, both from the same town attending Harding at the same time, and both majoring in music, were deeply in love. Soon after the school year began, the young man died in an automobile accident. The young woman began to pine and grieve; the only way that she could comfort herself was to go up to one of the private practice rooms on the third floor and play the piano and sometimes sing.

Soon afterwards, she too died, apparently from loneliness and grief, before the first semester was even over. Years passed, and people say they still hear her playing on the third floor.

But what makes it mysterious is that since the year she died, the old music building has been torn down, and a new one built in its place. When you stand on the second floor of the new building some nights, you can hear her playing above you.

Even though the new music building is only two stories tall.

THE GHOST OF ELLA BARHAM

IT SEEMS THAT GHOSTS MOST OFTEN WALK in the place where they were murdered. They most often haunt a place where they died by violence, or mutilation, or without warning. Fox hunters and 'coon hunters on Crooked Creek, near the Killebrew Ford, about eighteen miles below Harrison, Arkansas, say they still see the ghost of Ella Barham, dressed all in white, walking near the mine shaft where the body was found.

On November 21, 1912, Ella went out riding near our house; her horse came back without her. That night, hunters spotted a herd of hogs loudly rooting around some suspicious looking objects under a loose pile of rocks near an abandoned mine shaft. It was a corpse, cut into pieces by a saw. There were signs the body had been carried over Crooked Creek by the murderer, who must have surprised her on the road.

A young man named Odus Davidson was suspected of the crime from the start, even though he joined in the search for the girl before her body was found. A local justice of the peace believed that Odus had been jilted by Ella not long before. The day afterward, the local judge swore out a warrant for Odus's arrest. At his family's house, when the posse came to get him, Odus jumped out a back window and fled to the woods. He had peppered his socks to keep bloodhounds from trailing him.

They soon caught up with him, though, and he was taken without resistance. He admitted that he was cutting wood near the place Ella had last been seen but denied that he had murdered Ella.

The flight, the peppered socks, the presumed jilting, his admission of being near the death scene, my report that he had come through my yard not long after the murder, and the additional claim that there was blood on his socks when he was caught, was enough to sway the jury towards conviction. We deliberated a short time and returned a guilty verdict. Odus Davidson was hanged just before the Arkansas death penalty was changed to electrocution at the state penitentiary's death house. Odus Davidson was the last man hanged legally in Arkansas.

The body of the victim had been cut up horribly, into seven pieces, but the ghost the hunters claim they see down on Crooked Creek is all in one piece. The prosecutor at the trial had quoted Bible verses, and turned to Odus, shouting, "And where is Ella Barham?"

I guess the answer could be, "Still down at Crooked Creek, near Pleasant Ridge."

VI. HAINTS AND HOLLERS

"Haints" are haunts and "hollers" are the hollows—
the coves, or deep, narrow valleys of the Ozarks.
Haints are just naturally fond of hollers, it seems.

FROZEN CHARLOTTE

CHARLOTTE WAS A LOVELY YOUNG THING, dressed in all the finest. And she couldn't abide to be unfashionable. She held her head high and wore her dresses proud'. And all the young menfolk admired her something awful.

She was brazen to her family, and talked back to her mother when there was a dance planned at the schoolhouse and her mother warned her not to go. There'd be liquor at a dance, not like at an honest play-party. And at a dance, guns were sometimes drawn and difficulties settled by violence. But the finest fiddler in the Ozarks was set to play this dance, and Charlotte wouldn't've missed it for the whole wide world.

She dressed in her finest silk dress, with her velvet coat and matching muff and bonnet, and called for her servant man to drive her to the schoolhouse on the coldest night of the winter.

Now the snow was as thick as a man's hand, with a coat of ice on top, and no wagon could make the hills. The old servant dragged the cutter out of the shed, a low sled with high wooden walls and short, low runners of pine. He hitched one good bay horse to the cutter, and went in to get Charlotte.

As Charlotte left the cabin, her mother gave the servant a quilt to cover with, and he thanked her. She handed a quilt to Charlotte, but Charlotte refused.

"I'll not been seen in a country quilt!" she snapped.

The old man helped Charlotte to sit in the cutter on a tapestry cushion from the rocking chair in the parlor. He knelt in the front of the cutter, in his quilt, and clucked to the horse to go.

The wind was kicking up as the cutter clattered out of the house yard into the darkness. The open sky above was dusted with thousands of scattered stars like broken glass. The mother looked worried, in the door of the cabin, as the cutter disappeared in the blackness.

"Oh, I' never known it so cold," said the servant.

"Drive on," said Charlotte coldly.

The cutter slid along the ice, the horse's hooves cracking and the runner crunching. The world looked like a broken mirror, sharp and sparkling.

"Ain't you cold, Charlotte, honey?"

The wind slit through the trees, and cut the words into pieces.

"Drive *on!*"

The old man was chilled to the bone, and scared about how lightly and fashionably Charlotte was dressed, but he dared not look back, for Charlotte could be cruel when she chose. After a long while, as the cutter drew near the schoolhouse, the old man spoke again.

"We' almost there, Charlotte!"

"Drive on!"

Terror seized the old man.

He cracked the whip and shook the reins, and drove the horse like wind through the icy night. The cutter struck branches drooping with icicles and brushed them off to shatter on the frozen road. The wind began to keen like a dying animal and the horse snorted steam and spat bullets of ice as he thundered along with the cutter flying and the runners singing.

The old man pulled the cutter into the warm light of the schoolhouse windows. People inside were drinking and laughing and dancing to the squall of the fiddle. The old man climbed off the front of the cutter and hurried, stumbling in his quilt wrap, to help Charlotte out the back.

Some menfolk inside heard the snorting, stamping horse, and came to the door. They saw the old servant standing behind the cutter, rocking and shaking his head. They came out to the cutter and looked at Charlotte. She sat on the cushion, straight and cold, her hands folded in her muff.

Her eyes were wide and staring, shimmering like glass, with a layer of ice. Her lips were tightly closed and dusted with a white gloss of frost.

The men stood and stared until they finally understood why she did not greet them.

There in the cutter, dressed to kill, was stylish Charlotte frozen cold and dead.

If you dare to drive your wagon or your automobile in the bitter cold wind of midwinter, through a lashing ice storm in the dark Ozark hollers, beware the voice that drives men mad.

Beware a voice behind you in the blackness of the back seat, like the cracking of ice.

"Drive on!"

THE LEGEND OF VIVIA THOMAS

THERE IS A STRANGE GRAVE MARKER in the cemetery where my father is buried, in Fort Gibson, Oklahoma. In the Circle of Honor is the grave of the only woman ever to serve as a man in the cavalry. Vivia Thomas had fallen in love with a young man back East where they both lived. When he joined the Army and was sent West to Indian territory, she secretly followed him, suspecting that he would not be faithful to her.

She dressed as fair young man and enlisted in the same fort as her lover. No one recognized her as a woman. He didn't recognize her, since he never expected to see her there. Sure enough, she found that he was spending time in the home of a local Indian girl, even though he had been engaged to Vivia when he went West. She became enraged with a desire for revenge.

On a December night in 1869 she waited by the road near the local girl's home, and as shot her former lover as he rode by, she shot him with a rifle. The Army assumed that the Indians had killed the lieutenant to keep him away from the girl he was seeing.

No one would have ever suspected, except for the fact that Vivia began to see the dead lieutenant's ghost, visiting her each night, filling her with grief and remorse. She confessed the killing to a chaplain, and began to sit nightly by her dead lover's grave and cry. She froze to death on January 7, 1870, a victim of the bitter cold, of bitter remorse, and of the visitations of the ghost of her former lover, murdered by her own hand.

I CAN'T GET IN!

MY GRANDDADDY GREW UP in Newton County, Arkansas. He's dead now, but when I was a boy he told me this story. He and a friend had been to a dance, and had gotten drunk on moonshine. It was real strong stuff, and both boys were sick and staggering. They lived side by side, and were walking each other home, trying to stay standing up on the road.

They came to the graveyard and knew they could short-cut through it. They got about halfway through, and the other boy got sick and sat down on a grave to let his head stop spinning. Granddaddy went on. About five minutes later, the other boy ran past Granddaddy like he was standing still. Granddaddy ran crazily, trying to keep up, and when he got to the other boy's front porch there he was, shaking like a leaf and stone cold sober.

"What happened?" asked Granddaddy.

"I was sitting on that grave," said the other boy, "and somebody started poking me on the shoulder. I looked up. It was a skeleton, standing beside me, poking me on the shoulder and saying, `I can't get in. You're in my way! I can't get in!'"

Granddaddy swore it was the truth.

STILL ON PATROL

OUTSIDE SPRINGFIELD, MISSOURI, is a battlefield park that enshrines the area of the battle the Yankees call Wilson's Creek. To the Confederates, who won this engagement and killed Union General Lyons in the fight, this event was known as The Battle of Oak Hills.

These days, the oak trees stand calm, and the field is wide and open, even more open and rolling than it was the year of the battle. Cannons stand in typical battlefield park positions, and re-enactors come frequently to this place to show new generations what the battles of the War Between the States were like.

But late at night, for anyone still on the parks grounds, there is one soldier whose tattered Confederate drab uniform is not a reproduction. He has been seen off and on for decades. He walks a picket in one corner of the battlefield. He can only be seen from a distance; if you approach him, he vanishes.

He's a ghost.

And he's still on patrol over one hundred and forty years later.

THE BURNING BRIDE

IN FAYETTEVILLE, ARKANSAS, the old folks tell the gruesome tale of the burning bride in Judge Walker's wood lot. Judge Walker was an Arkansas Supreme Court Justice, and in the early 1870s he built a brick mansion on East Mountain for his daughter and son-in-law. The local folks they hired as servants wouldn't stay at the house after dark—they soon learned why.

At the end of the War Between the States, a young couple from Fort Smith moved into a log house on the same parcel of land as Judge Walker's house. On their wedding night the young bride, still in her wedding dress, bent over the fireplace to stoke the fire. The hem of her dress caught fire. This wasn't unusual in olden days, and a young woman would just pat the fire out on the hem of a calico dress. But this wedding dress was Venetian lace, and the flame shot up the overlay to the bodice. The young girl panicked and ran outside. The wind fanned the flames, and she ran screaming through the underbrush of the wood lot out back. The brush caught fire, and took the woods and her life.

The old folks still claim to hear the distant cries of the burning bride, or to see the dim glow of her burning dress out in the wood lot that still stands behind the house.

When I lived on East Mountain in the 1960s, I thought I might have heard the burning bride, too. But then again it may have been that eighty-pound basset hound down the block.

THE FIDDLER IN FARALONE CAVE

EVERY CAVE IN THE OZARKS has two or three names, because one group of folks will come by and name it, and move on, and the next folks to come along give it a different name. One of the prettiest waterfalls in a cave is Eden Falls in Eden Cave at Lost Valley. But there are others, too. One of the biggest caves ever used for dancing is at Bella Vista, Arkansas; there was a speakeasy there during Prohibition. But other caves were used as dancing halls as well.

One cave was called Faralone Cave, and it had a wide bluff shelter as its mouth, and a deep passage to an underground stream that led down to Faralone Falls, far and alone in its depths. It was cool and dry in the cave mouth, and the deep passage provided a place to sneak off and have a snort of moonshine whiskey or a sweet word with your gal.

The finest fiddle player in that part of the Ozarks played almost every night at Faralone Cave, and many a girl fell in love with the handsome young man. One young girl, though, was the one he wanted to dance with, and she didn't seem to pay him much heed.

When she turned up at dance after dance with a young farmer from across the river, the fiddler knew his chance at her love was gone. Finally one night, during the break, he went back into the passage to get a long drink. He sat and played his fiddle sadly as he drank the clear moonshine flavored with walnut bark. When he got up, he was reeling, and not because of the music, either. He must have gone the wrong way, toting his candle and his fiddle.

When the fiddler wasn't back, and the sun was coming up, some of the young bucks that didn't go to church went back and spent all day Sunday searching the cave for him.

Ever' once in a while, they thought they could hear his fiddle playing in the distance, but they never could find him. They went back and forth past the falls, down each arm of the cave they knew about, and never found a thing.

They quit having dances there, because when someone else would play the fiddle out front, and someone else would go back into the deep passage to get a swig of 'shine, they'd come running out a few minutes later swearing they'd heard another fiddler playing a different tune deep in the cave. Folks got so scared of the fiddler's ghost and his ghost fiddle that they quit going around there anymore.

You can go there today and still hear him playing his fiddle. Anyone can direct you to the cave. Only now it's not called Faralone Cave anymore.

Most folks call it Fiddler's Cave.

THE GHOST IS STILL MAD

THE GHOST THAT BROUGHT both shivers and grins was told about in both Arkansas and Missouri, which means it must have happened in both states. Up in Missouri, it is said to have happened in Stone County, near Yokum Pond.

There was an old man and an old woman who lived in a cabin, and they just hollered and cussed at each other all the time. She threw pots at him and he kicked the furniture around. They'd argue about the weather and the cooking and the sermon they'd heard the one time they went to church and the upcoming election. They yelled and screamed and said every word anyone in the valley had ever heard and one or two they must have made up themselves.

Folks could hardly sleep at night and dared not walk by most days for all the awful racket them two kicked up. They threatened to kill each other about seven times a day, so when the old woman died, the sheriff came in and searched the cabin pretty good, and looked all over the body with the doctor's help, to see iffen she'd been murdered.

Well, she'd just up and died, of orneriness no doubt, and hadn't been murdered, so they buried her and things were quiet for thirteen days.

Then, strangely enough, when folks walked by the cabin, they could hear the old woman, still screaming and yelling, and every once in a while, a pan would come crashing out a windowpane.

Only one person ever dared to stop by and see who was doing all the yelling, and he said the voice sounded like it come from the bottom of a deep barrel. He asked who was doing all the cussing and spitting.

The old man blushed. "Well, it's the ghost of my wife," he said. "But it's alright. She ain't mad at anybody but me."

A pan came out the door, and the young man ran away.

THE GHOST AT VIRGIN'S BLUFF

ALONG THE JAMES RIVER in Stone and Taney Counties in Missouri, early Spanish explorers came in the 1760s looking for legendary silver. Some people say they found it, a rich vein, near where the community of Branson West sits at the junction of Missouri highways 76 West and 13. Either the Spaniards made their camp on Breadtray Mountain for defense, or perhaps that is where the vein was located. Either way, modern deer hunters trek across the same *azafate*—breadtray—that was once a Spanish mining camp or fortress.

There is a story, told among the descendants of the earliest English-speaking settlers of that part of Stone County, around the county seat at Galena. How the story survived is unclear. It might have been told among the local Delaware Indians, and passed along to the English-speaking American settlers that came in after the Louisiana Purchase in 1804. The story goes like this:

Among the Spanish was a young soldier named Esteban; his *capitán* did not send Esteban to work in the mines, but preferred that he stand guard and patrol the slopes of Breadtray Mountain where the camp was located. In one of his patrols, off to the high bluffs along the James River, Esteban met a young Indian woman, the daughter of the chief of the Deleware tribe, named Moon Flower, or possibly Moon Song.

They fell in love at first sight, and they arranged to meet secretly as often as possible after that. They met at the edge of a bluff where no one could sneak up and surprise them. No one could climb the bluff, and anyone coming up the gentle slope from the other way could be clearly seen by the young lovers. If a Delaware approached, Moon Flower began to gather berries, and Esteban hid in the underbrush. If Spaniards approached, Moon Flower hid, and Esteban practiced swordplay on the berry canes, or knelt in prayer with his missal.

The Indian people, who had come to this area from the East to escape contact with the Europeans, resented the way the Spanish plundered the land, taking all the silver at once. The Indians would have used only the silver they needed each generation. They began to plan an attack to wipe out the Spaniards.

By coincidence, the Spanish *capitán* also planned an escape, by night, when the Delawares were forbidden by their religion to fight.

Each young lover learned of his or her people's plans, and their last meeting was a sad one as they warned each other of what was to come. Moon Flower wanted Esteban to stay with her; Esteban wanted Moon Flower to go with him back to Nueva Orleanes.

In the end, Esteban promised to return within one year to meet Moon Flower again.

And so, by night, the Spanish moved down the trail off Breadtray Mountain, their ox cart wheels freshly greased with bear fat, and the men marching out of step for quiet. At dawn the Delawares attacked the campsite of the Spaniards and looked with despair at the empty tents and abandoned campfires.

At the bluff above the James, Moon Flower stood alone on the edge, looking out to the south, watching the end of the caravan wend its way back to Louisiana.

Three hundred sixty-five days Moon Flower came to the bluff to watch for Esteban to return. He never came back. On the 366th morning, she walked to the bluff and did not stop at the edge. She walked out into the air, and fell in her white buckskin like the falling petals of a white catalpa blossom, two hundred feet to the rocks below.

The Delaware chieftain found his daughter, broken on the rocks, and ordered seven days' prayer and fasting before her body was burned in a funeral pyre. The medicine man put a curse on the bluff of the virgin Indian chieftainess, and none of the Delaware people went there again.

In the two centuries that passed afterwards, that bend in the James River was the site of more keelboat wrecks than any other. Those who passed that water route by night claimed to hear the low moaning of the Delaware medicine man, or the high wail of the long-dead virgin, perhaps as she fell, because the sounds seemed to come from above the passersby, up the wall of the bluff.

When Table Rock Dam closed in the valley to make Table Rock Lake in the late 1950s, more tourists' cameras misfired, more trotlines got snarled, and more picnickers got ants in their pants at that one lonely bluff above the lake. Anyone who camped or fished there at night still heard the faint, high wail of the virgin of the bluff. Some night fishermen almost broke their necks looking suddenly up the bluff when they saw reflected in the water the white form of the falling ghost. Maybe it was the moon. Maybe it was Moon Flower.

The legend reached its thundering climax a few years ago, when there was a high wailing sound deep in the night, and the thousand-ton stone bluff crumbled into Table Rock Lake, ending forever the sight and the sound of the ghost of Virgin's Bluff.

THE GHOST DOOR

MY GRANDPA AND GRANDMA BOUGHT A HOUSE over in Newton County, Arkansas, not too many years back. An old man had died in one of the bedrooms, and Grandpa left that room more or less empty, just for storage. It had a solid wooden door that wouldn't stay closed. He would shut the door every night, and the plunger would click, but about midnight the plunger would click again and the door would swing slowly open.

The hinges needed oiling, and the door would creak.

Some nights it scared Grandma and Grandpa pretty bad.

Grandpa decided to oil the hinges and put one of those screen-door latches with an eye hook on the door. He put the eye hook into the frame and shut the door. It clicked the same as always, and he latched the latch.

About midnight the plunger clicked and woke Grandpa up.

Then he heard the latch drop against the door, loose from its eye hook.

Then he heard the door creak open, the same as always.

He got up the next morning and unscrewed the latch and eye hook and threw them away. He left the door standing ajar that night, and every night after that, and they were never awakened again.

THE GHOST AT HUGHES

AT HUGHES, ARKANSAS, TWO BROTHERS, James and John, lived in a house that they had been told was haunted. The previous owner, an old man, claimed that his dead wife haunted the house. When he died, the house went up for sale. After the brothers bought the house, the ghost of the wife was seen for the first time by people other than the old man. She always wore a long, white gown; she had died young and was very pretty for a ghost.

One afternoon the brothers came home from working in the soybean fields, and they were walking toward the refrigerator for a soda. A friend of theirs, who had come home with them, looked down a hallway from the kitchen, and he saw a woman pass by, and he dropped his drink. It scared him, because he knew the house should have been empty, and he asked James and John who was home besides them. They said, "Nobody's here," but he swore up and down that he'd seen a woman in a long white gown. That old boy left for home shortly after that.

Jim and John both just laugh about this story, because even though the house is haunted, they've lived there long enough to know this haunt wasn't going to hurt them. They'd become comfortable with the idea of a ghost in their house. Several times the ghost had appeared; they had seen her, other guests at the place had seen her. But finally even the brothers were scared by the lady in the white gown.

One day their father had come home. He thought his wife was around the house, and doing some work upstairs. He could hear her footsteps upstairs, and he called up, "I'm just going to get a sandwich and go back to the fields." His wife didn't answer, but he heard her moving around upstairs. In a few minutes he called up, "I'm going back out now, Honey." He could hear her rocking chair upstairs rocking. Then his wife walked in the front door. She'd gone to town and come back.

They ran upstairs and opened the door to the sewing room. The rocking chair was still rocking, but it was empty. That scared their father, and after that, the whole family was not so comfortable as they'd been before to share their home with the lady in the long, white gown.

THE GHOST AT GINGER BLUE

ON THE ELK RIVER IN SOUTHWEST MISSOURI, not far from Cowskin Landing, is a place called Ginger Blue. A Revolutionary War veteran named Ginger Blue, a Delaware Indian, is buried there. The nearby tourist lodge also took its name from the great warrior. Around the lodge, they tell the story of a ghost that has appeared at a nearby cave. The legend, at least one version of it, runs like this:

Ginger Blue moved west with his Revolutionary War pension, and settled on land at the westernmost edge of white settlement, as far into the trackless Indian lands as he could get without severing ties to the river trade and hunting and trapping that brought European people into the area. It is said he operated a lodge for these travelers, and made his living as a hosteler.

The Indian people came to the lodge also, to trade and to visit. Ginger Blue's daughter fell in love with one of these young men, but his tribe and hers did not intermarry (or perhaps their two fathers objected to the marriage). Still they saw each other frequently, and were allowed by her father to visit quietly near the Elk River by the mouth of a cave.

One day, at the cave mouth, the young Indian woman was waiting for her lover, when suddenly an angry mother bear came out of the cave. She had apparently moved in there a day or two before, while the young lovers were away, and now charged the Indian woman whom she considered a threat to her cubs.

Before the sow bear had a chance to sink her teeth into the woman, the young man arrived for their visit. He pulled his knife from his belt and gave a war cry. The sow bear turned on him, and they fought tooth and claw.

Both man and bear were bleeding furiously as the sow turned and re-entered the cave. Fearing her return, the man plunged into the darkness after her. The young woman was unable to stop him. The war cries and bear howls echoed from deep within the cave for a long time before all was silent. Neither man nor bear ever came out.

The cave was so tortuously twisted, and so deep, that Indians with torches gave up before they ever found the bodies of the beast and the warrior. The cubs ran from the cave when the men with torches came, but no one killed them, fearing one of them might be carrying the warrior's spirit.

Although the search party gave up after a few hours, the young woman never gave up. She became known as Bear Warrior's Woman, and sat at the mouth of the cave in eternal vigil for the man she had loved. Where she cried, some said her tears weathered the rock into the face of the young man who died defending her. Others said the young man's spirit came out to her one night, to give his permission for her to end her vigil after many years. They say his ghost lay down beside the woman, who had taken to sleeping at the cave mouth.

Where he lay, with his head on the rock, his ghostly image melted into the rock forever. She was buried in the cave at the end of her life, and now his image stands vigil for her.

He's the ghost at Ginger Blue.

THE GHOST AT THE CONFEDERATE GRAVEYARD

ON A SMALL HILL IN FAYETTEVILLE, ARKANSAS, stands a tiny cemetery, surrounded by an octagonal wall. The monument in the center is to the unknown Confederate dead from several nearby battles at Elkhorn Tavern, Prairie Grove and other skirmishes. But across the old road, up the hill in the vine-tangled woods, there are other grave markers and headstones. These are for the family and friends, even camp followers, who died years later and asked to be buried near the Confederate monument.

Two of my college professors lived up near that Confederate graveyard and its jumbled companion, and while one swore there were ghosts there, the other denied it.

More than one person, however, who has gone up along the old road to "park" swears to have seen something ghostly and white moving in among the vines and tangled trees.

Some say it is the ghost of a Confederate soldier who leaves his grave to visit his camp-follower lover, who is buried in the woods. Others turn the legend the other way and say it is the woman who rises by night and travels to the monument, looking for her man, who may rest there or in an unmarked grave in the national or state parks at the battlefields.

People who have seen the figure, unidentifiable as it is, swear it is real. People with and without their college degrees.

THE GHOST OF NICKERSON RIDGE

THE OLD WILDERNESS ROAD south from Springfield, Missouri, ran along the ridges in what was then western Taney County (now Stone County) and led down a winding path to the Kimberling Ferry crossing of the White River (now spanned by a modern bridge over the deep waters of Table Rock Lake at Kimberling City). Missouri 13—an ominous number—follows that roadbed today.

Since the pioneer times, travelers along this road have claimed to see a headless ghost along a very short section of the old trail. On rainy nights, the spirit keeps to the brush alongside the road, and moves parallel to the traveler, sometimes growling like a panther or moaning like a dying creature. On dark nights the growls may be heard, even if the thing cannot be seen.

But it is on clear nights, with a sliver of moon, that the thing is seen most clearly. Usually it looks out from behind a tree trunk at a passerby, or comes partway out of the brush at the side of the road to terrify riders and spook their horses. Passengers in slower-moving automobiles early in the twentieth century have seen the headless ghost, and described it as being the size and shape of a man, walking stooped over. He is dressed in black clothes and may be wearing a cape or a loose coat.

And he has no head.

The most famous sighting of the Ghost of Nickerson Ridge was back in 1915. Tomp Turner lived near the Kimberling Bridge on the White River, and was not counted as a superstitious man. He had even declared that he did not believe in the headless ghost. Then, one night, he was riding south on horseback along the Wilderness Road toward home. His horse began to stamp and shy to the side. When he looked down the road ahead he saw it.

Coming toward him along the road was the headless ghost, gliding along as if floating just above the roadbed. When it got within fifty feet, the horse broke and crashed into the brush at the side of the road. When Tomp got the horse back on the road, another fifty feet along, the ghost was nowhere to be seen.

But, as Tomp later told Otto Ernest Rayburn, "I didn't go back to look for it!"

Tomp rode home as fast as he could, and he did not try to hide the fact that he had seen the headless haint on the Wilderness Road.

VII. GHOST JOKES

Some Ozark hill folks use the word "joke" to identify any story with a happy ending, but these spooky spoofs also have a chuckle at the end.

THE CORPSE RISES AGAIN

ON A COLD, DARK NIGHT, two graverobbers went into the burying ground and opened up a fresh-dug grave. They took out the corpse from its pine box, and loaded it into a wagon full of straw, to hide it.

This is how they made their living. They went around digging up the dead, and selling the bodies to some medical school up in Kansas City or somewhere. They'd leave the pine coffin in place, put all the fresh dirt back, and put all the flowers back on, so's no one would know there was anything amiss. And they'd be off up the road and get their twenty-five dollar gold piece for their evening's work.

The night turned nasty, and a cold rain mixed with snow came down like needles. The two graverobbers turned in at an inn for hot toddies.

While they were in the inn, the corpse lay under the straw in the wagon. After about an hour, a drunk country boy left the inn, staggering bad', and saw the wagon full of straw. It looked pretty good at the time, so the fellow climbed into the wagon bed and pulled a big pile of straw over himself as bedcovers. In a few minutes he was snoring, and in an hour he was stone-cold asleep, as silent as the dead man next to him.

After consuming a whole bottle of rum, one hot cup at a time, the two graverobbers came out of the inn carrying a bottle of whiskey as a chaser. One climbed onto the wagon seat in the cold rain, and the other untied the team from the hitchrack. Then he climbed on too and they rattled away with the dead man and the drunk in the straw.

After about three trips over the bedrock on a ridge road, the bouncing tossed the drunk high enough that he woke up on the drop.

As he stirred around in the wagon bed, the two drivers were sniffing and coughing and drinking the whiskey.

One of them held the bottle back over the straw as a joke, and said, "Rise up, old stiff, and have a snort of whiskey."

Thinking they were talking to him, the young drunk rose up and reached out his hand. "Thank ye kindly," he said. "Don't mind iffen I do."

Well, the two graverobbers dropped offen both sides of the wagon seat and were in the next county by sunup.

The young drunk finished the whiskey and took the wagon home. The sheriff took over from there, and the relatives of the dead man gave him an even bigger funeral with the money they found in the dashboard, where the robbers'd dropped it. Not many men get two big funerals, even here in Christian County.

SKIN AND BONES

There was an old woman,
She was just skin and bones,
Oh, oh, oh-oo!
There was an old woman,
She was just skin and bones,
Oh, oh, oh-oo!
Well, she looked up and she looked down,
She spied a corpse upon the ground,
Oh, oh, oh-oo!
She went to the parson and she said,
Will I look so when I am dead?
Oh, oh, oh-o-o?
And the parson said,
[scream] Yes!

IT'S COLD IN THE GRAVE

A DRUNK WAS WALKING HOME from the moonshine still and wandered into the graveyard by mistake. He wandered right into an open grave that was waiting to be filled the next day. He tried to climb out, but he couldn't. He finally laid down and fell asleep. The next morning, another drinker came in early to get a seat for the funeral. The noise he was making woke up the drunk in the grave. He was shivering from the cold.

"Lordy, I'm cold," hollered out the drunk.

The other drinker looked into the grave and said, "Well, no wonder you're cold, you've kicked all your covers off."

YOU CAN'T GET OUT!

SO THERE WAS THIS FELLER who liked his whiskey, and he was on his way to the house after a dance where he had drunk his fill. He was weaving pretty badly down the road, and sidled off through the graveyard as a shortcut. There was to be a funeral the next day, and the grave was already dug, with the dirt piled up beside it.

The drunk didn't see it coming, and he walked straight off into the grave. Being drunk and all, he wasn't hurt at all, but he got real sober real quick in that cold grave.

He scrambled and scrabbled and tried to climb out, but the walls were too steep and too crumbly. After about an hour of trying, he just sat back down in the grave and waited for dawn, figuring the funeral director would be along soon enough and pull him out before the owner of the plot came along to lie in it.

Well, most of the night passed, and along came another feller who had been at the dance, who was weaving around even worse than the first, and he crossed that graveyard and went headlong into that hole that hadn't been there the day before.

The second feller scrambled and scrabbled and couldn't get out, and the first feller, trying to be helpful, finally said in a calm voice:

"You know, you can't get out of this here grave."

But the second feller did!

STEALING PAWPAWS

IT WAS AUTUMN, AND TWO BOYS had been out stealing pawpaws from under a neighbor's tree. Their families didn't have good pawpaw trees, and the fruit was just ripe, so they waited until the fellow with the good tree was out milking, and they crept into his yard and stole a whole bagful. Since there were two boys and only one sack, they had to divide up the goods. They figured that since it was sundown the least likely place for them to be disturbed was the graveyard.

So they went to the graveyard, and hid behind a big tall head marker just inside the rock wall, and started dividing up the pawpaws, saying,

"You take this one, I'll take that one."

While they were counting, this big old cornfed country boy came swinging along the road whistling to himself. He stopped just as he got alongside the boys on the back of the wall. He heard them real clearly saying,

"You take this one, I'll take that one."

It scared that country boy to death. He took off running all the way to the house. When he got to the porch, he hollered,

"Pop! Pop! I heard them! It was the Lord and the Devil, out in the graveyard dividing up the souls!"

By the time he got inside the house, his father said,

"Son, you've been in the liquor again, haven't you?"

"No, Pop, really!" said the boy, jumping up and down with excitement. "I heared them dividing up the souls, going `You take this one, I'll take that one!' Really I did!"

"Son," said the old man, "if you heard that, I want to hear it, too."

"Well, come on, let's go!" said the boy, starting out the door.

"Son," said the old man, "you know I ain't stirred a step with the rheumatism these ten solid years. You'll have to carry me. That's what I raised you big old boys for. Pick me up and carry me down there."

So the great big boy grabbed the skinny old man and set him on his shoulders, and off they went to the graveyard. As they got closer and closer the boy went slower and slower, until he was creeping up on the graveyard wall, old man and all. Those two boys were still there, but they were through dividing up the good pawpaws, and were down to the last two.

Just as the country boy and the old man got to the wall and leaned over to listen, one of the thieves said,

"There's not but these two left. You take that big fat one and I'll take the old shriveled-up one."

That was it! The country boy reared back and threw his old gray-haired father off, and lit out running toward the house. And his pop, who hadn't stirred a step with the rheumatism for ten solid years, beat the boy home by a full minute!

RED LIGHT

ON THE OUTSKIRTS OF JONESBORO, ARKANSAS, there is a mysterious grave haunted by a ghostly light of a very rare nature and color. College boys at ASU (Arkansas State University) often take their dates to "park" beside the cemetery, where they can scare their date with the obviously true story that explains the ghostly light.

The area is lonely and secluded, and many old stones and monuments rise high into the night among dark, twisted trees and sinister shrubbery. The ghostly light is easy to spot, and unique in all the ghostlore because this light is red! You see, it's the grave of a prostitute, buried almost a century ago.

The white monument from which the ghost light shines is an obelisk, standing tall in the midst of other smaller stones that are more modern. The brazen hussy won't be still even in death, because if you park just in the right place, near a moss-covered monument carved from marble in the shape of a tree trunk, felled by the Grim Reaper, you can catch a glimpse of a pale red light, glowing from the orb at the top of the obelisk.

But if you bring a date to this spot you must be careful to keep her attention on the graveyard, because if she looks directly opposite the graveyard on the other side of the road, she will notice the tall radio transmitter tower with the huge red light on it. The ghostly light is a romantic hoax.

THE HAINTED CAR

THE PREACHER 'AS SETTIN' IN THE CHURCH HOUSE, long after ever'one else had gone home, waitin' for the fire in the stove to die out, readin' his Bible. It was cold and dark, an' the wind howled aroun' the ol' wood-frame church, bangin' the shutters. The preacher, he scattered the coals in the ash, turned the damper, and closed the stove; blew out the coal oil lamps an' latched the shutters.

It 'as Halloween night; fell on a Sunday that year. Preacher swung shut the door to the church and turned the ol' iron key. Now, he weren't a superstitious feller, but he plumb shuddered in that wind as he pulled his coat up tight and commenced to walk down the rock road to the farmhouse where he was stayin' the night.

He had to go over one hillock an' through two hollers to get to where he's goin', and on the hillock stood the graveyard. Down in the first holler, he thought he heard somethin' on the road a-hind 'im. He stopped and turned to look, but there weren't no moon, an' it was as dark as the inside of a cow. He walked on. A minute later, climbin' toward the graveyard, he thought he heard somethin' ag'in! He stopped an' turned back to listen. He couldn't hear no hooves, nor trace chains janglin', so he knowed it weren't no wagon. He couldn't hear no engine runnin', so he figured t'weren't no car.

He walked on, an' just afore the edge of the graveyard, he heard it ag'in: a low sound, like somethin' horribl' heavy, stalkin' 'im slow, crunchin' rock underfoot as it come. Somethin' big an' dark moved up the road at 'im, bigger'n a bear!

He backed a coupl' steps, then turned an' was about to run for it, when the thing come up against the sky an' he seen it. It 'as a automobile, but without its lanterns lit, movin' slower'n he'd ever seen one move, an' makin' no sound at'all.

The hainted car come up on him slow', an' stopped aside 'im.

"Well," thought Preacher, "it's some deacon on 'is way back from takin' some sister home, an' he's offerin' me a ride!" He stepped up to the car, opened the door an' got in, and leaned up to thank the driver.

The car was empty, 'cept for him.

Slowly, it commenced to move past the cemetery, no sound but the crush of gravels under its wheels. At the big iron gate to the graveyard, it stopped!

"Well," thought Preacher, "I guess this is where I get out!"

He climbed out of the car, an' stepped back to the gate, lookin' from side to side. All o' sudden, he heard somethin' a-hin' the nearest stone, breathin' hard an' growly-like. Slowly, Preacher walked aroun' the headstone. There stood a deacon o' the church, pantin' an' blowin' like somethin' 'as wrong with 'im.

"Brother Dan," said Preacher, "don't go near that car! There's somethin' wrong about it!"

"I know, Brother John," said Brother Dan, "I been pushin' the damn thing a mile!"

Glossary

Arkansas: the name Arkansas is pronounced Arkansaw. It most likely derives from the French phrase *aux Kansas,* which when used in a sentence would mean "over in the land of the Kansaw Indians," referring to the modern Kaw tribe. Although there was controversy over the pronunciation in 1840 (whether to end with "sass" or "saw"), there was no doubt in anyone's mind in the late 1700s and early 1800s. Letters from Washington to the Territory always used the spelling (and pronunciation) "Arkansaw." The confusion was generated by the publisher of the *Arkansas Gazette,* oldest newspaper west of the Mississippi founded in 1816, who chose the French spelling ("Arkansas") over the original English spelling ("Arkansaw"). The compromise made at the time of statehood (1836) was to use the French spelling but keep the correct French and English pronunciation (ending in "saw"), which has confused generations since, and will continue to do so.

bald knob: a treeless, but usually grass-covered knob. See *knob.*

blight: any force, monster or witchcraft that destroys hope and blanks out goodness. Plant or animal epidemics, or any disease or unexplainable tragedy.

Bloody Bones: a dancing skeleton in African-American folklore, a part of Old Raw Head in Ozark folklore, but a separate distinct monster in English folklore.

booger: a monster, especially an oversized spirit-animal. Some Ozarkers say "booger," some say "bugger." Also, the "boogieman" or the "bogeyman;" from the same root word as the British "boggan," but not the same creature.

catywhompus: (or kittywhompus) on a diagonal rather than perpendicular. Dovetailed log structures will lean to an incredible degree before collapsing with age.

cove: in Ozark parlance, a narrow, steep-walled valley with a spring or waterfall at the head, which usually falls swiftly to a larger valley at the cove mouth. On Ozark lakes, locals also use the word "cove" as it is widely known, to mean a small, enclosed arm of the lake.

dasn't: archaic for "dare not" or "dared not."

et: archaic for "ate" or "eaten."

Faralone Cave: Possibly Bear Den Cave in Stone County, Missouri, now under Table Rock Lake. A fictitious cave in Stone, Taney, or Howell counties in Missouri.

fiddle: Ozark and American slang for violin.

Fiddler's Cave: almost any cave in which dances were once held to beat the summer heat. No specific Fiddler's Cave is known to these editors.

flatlanders: people who live outside the Ozarks (which are surrounded by plains, prairies, delta, and swamp). People from outside must come from flat land (if they live nearby).

ghost light: see *spook light.*

gowerow: (or gower, or gowrow) a mythological monster unique to the Ozarks, variously described as a pachyderm with horns bristling out of his back, or as we believe more accurately, an alligator-like critter ten to thirty feet long with a row of spikes down its spine. The name rhymes with "How now, brown cow." We maintain that the name is derived from the Anglo-Saxon words *gaer-raew* (spear-row). See *Ozark Tall Tales,* p. 27. Other Missourians maintain the word comes from the French word *garou,* meaning roughly "were-" as in werewolf (see "were-" in Glossary listing) or *loup garou,* with the modern pronunciation coming from a misreading of the French spelling using English phonetics. For further description see *We Always Lie to Strangers,* p. 41-6. See *The Talking Turtle,* p. 55 for a variant of Story No. 22, and *Ozark Tall Tales,* p. 23 for a folklorically accurate drawing that the illustrator made about twice as large as the gowerow is described in the story. See also *Ozarks Country,* p. 54. Gowerows were reportedly seen and even caught in Boone and Searcy Counties in Arkansas, and in Stone and Taney Counties in Missouri, and as far north as Washington County, Missouri.

haint: Ozark spelling/pronunciation of "haunt." See *haunt.*

hainted: Ozark variant of "haunted."

Halloweeners: celebrants of Halloween, trick-or-treaters. See *Down in the Holler,* p. 54.

haunt: as a noun, a spirit or ghost.

Heller, Lloyd "Shad": Blacksmith and actor, fictive mayor of Silver Dollar City theme park in Missouri, outside Branson. Deceased.

hog-scalding: a common autumn communal activity whereat hogs were slaughtered for winter provisions, the tough bristle hairs being scalded and scraped off the carcasses. A major gathering of neighbors for mutual assistance of the same folkloric stature as the better-known barn raisings and quilting bees.

holler: Ozark spelling/pronunciation of "hollow." The word holler, of course, also means "to yell"; the two meanings can be distinguished by their context. See *hollow*.

hollow: a narrow valley or deep depression in the terrain. There are thousands of hollows in the Ozarks, among the hills and knobs. See knob.

joke: Ozarkers use the word "joke" to mean any story with a happy ending, not necessarily a punch line or funny comment.

jularky: (or jularkie or jularker) female sweetheart. This is not an Ozark term, according to Randolph (in Deane's *Ozark Country*, p. 46) but is a common Appalachianism.

jump song: a song which ends with a fright for the listener, a song that makes the listener "jump," or in which the singer jumps at the listener in feigned attack.

knob: (sometimes spelled nob) a narrow, high hill with a capstone top, surmounted by a dirt dome. Knobs may be tree-covered or bald (without trees but grass-covered).

lie: Ozarkers use the word "lie" to mean joke, tall tale, any story that is ultimately not true.

locals: the local folks, the local inhabitants. Non-Ozarkers are usually called "furriners" (foreigners) or "flatlanders." Flatlanders pejoratively call Ozarkers "local yokels."

loess: fine, loamy deposits of soil left by rivers as sediment, then uplifted or cut deeper by the same river, creating gray, crumbling bluffs along the river.

Nickerson Ridge: a ridge five to six miles north of the White River (now part of Table Rock Lake) along the Old Wilderness Road (q.v.) north of the Kimberling Ferry in Missouri. The ridge now is the community of Stoneridge, where the editors of this collection live at this writing, and where The Headless Ghost used to roam.

Old Raw Head: a mythical monster who is either human or half human, and either headless or carries his head, depending on who is telling the story.

Old Walleyes: an Ozark booger, a monster, with dull, clouded (possibly blind) eyes. Perhaps a blind wildcat enlarged by legend. The creature is described variously as half-dog, half-cat, or part lion, part alligator, etc.

Old Wilderness Road: The Old Wilderness Road ran from Springfield, Missouri, south to the old Kimberling Ferry, passing through the area of Notch, and Nickerson Ridge before reaching the White River and crossing into Arkansas.

orance: although sometimes rendered "orange" by the press, and assumed to refer to golden fur, the word "orance" (rhymes with Lawrence) is a cat/man/monster often used as a joke on flatlanders. The orance is variously described as furry man, booger cat, or other vague monster. The orance is most often explained away as a lost collie (1940s), a lost pet lioness (1980s), or a tramp looking for a handout on a stormy night. The orance was most often seen around Reeds Spring, Missouri, in the Abesville area.

out-of-place animals: legendary animals that are often real creatures out of their rightful place. When we were new to Stone County, rumors circulated about an orange-furred booger cat; it prompted a new "flap" of tellings of booger animal stories. After a few weeks, the sheriff shot an illegally-owned and escaped pet lioness. Alligators are also not native to the Ozarks, but the appearance of one could give rise to legendary critters in other tales.

While the dragon of "St. George and the Dragon" is imagined in the United States as having been enormous, like Chinese dragons, contemporary Europeans pictured and carved the dragon as crocodile-sized. Since the Crusades had just returned from the Holy Land, where crocodiles are not unusual, the dragon may have been very real. Chinese dragons were perceived as enormous, but dinosaur bones exposed in sand and stone in Mongolia represent creatures of just the right dimensions. Those dragons may have been out-of-time instead of out-of-place. Ozark monsters like gowerows and booger dogs may somehow have natural explanations, just as dragons do.

Ozarks: the general region defined in the Introduction (pages 8-23). The name probably derives from the French phrase *aux arcs*, which, used in a sentence, would mean "over in the land of the bow makers," referring to the Quapaw or perhaps the Osage Indians.

Parler, Mary Celestia: See *Randolph, Mary Celestia Parler.*

pawpaw: (or papaw) [probably from papaya] a tree of the central and southern United States that bears a semi-sweet yellow-green-red fruit with numerous seeds. Ozarkers sometimes call them "Ozark bananas," although their shape is more reminiscent of a mango.

pennywinkle: a variant of periwinkle, a name applied to an Ozark flower by English and Scots-Irish settlers. In Britain, the flower is the *vinca major* and *vinca minor.*

Randolph, Mary Celestia Parler: Arkansas folklorist and collector (1904-1981), wife of Vance Randolph and instructor of folklore at the University of Arkansas at Fayetteville. Known as "Miss Parler" in Southern style feminism.

Randolph, Vance: Missouri folklorist (1892-1980) and author, later a guest lecturer at the University of Arkansas at Fayetteville.

raw head: the skinned head of an animal, usually a pig, to be smoked or cooked. The only part of the pig that was wasted was his squeal.

Rayburn, Otto Ernest: Arkansas folklorist and author (1891-1960), graduate of the University of Arkansas at Fayetteville.

razorback: the legendary wild hog of the Ozarks, supposedly so skinny and bony that its spine sticks out like a crosscut sawblade. Hill men supposedly turn the hogs on their backs and cut lumber with them.

sally-bally: a monster or stupid giant, malevolent in some stories, just vexing in others.

"Shad": a common nickname in the Ozarks, most famously applied to Lloyd Heller, actor and blacksmith, and fictive major of Silver Dollar City theme park for almost thirty years. Nickname for the Biblical Shadrach, who was one of the three captives to come out of the "fiery furnace" unharmed (Daniel 3: 11-17). "Shad" is often a blacksmith's nickname because of its association with that fiery furnace, which was presumably used to smelt gold for graven images.

so as: so that.

spook light: *ignis fatuus, feu folle,* foxfire, or some other haunting, unexplainable light, usually attributed to a ghost carrying a lantern, ghostly candles in a haunted house, etc.

still and all: nevertheless.

stone-cold: very much, as in stone-cold dead, and by extension in such phrases as "my stone-cold favorite."

Stone County: a county in Missouri along the White and James Rivers with extensive surviving Ozark culture and storytelling. Formerly part of larger Taney County. There is also a Stone County in the Arkansas Ozarks, but the stories in this collection that refer to Stone County refer to the Missouri locale.

Taney County: a county in Missouri along the White River with extensive surviving Ozark culture and storytelling.

'un: archaic for one, as in young one, loved one, etc. A politely impersonal pronoun, even used in introductions, such as "This 'un here is our beloved preacher man."

walleyes: blind-eyed, clouded-eyed, having eyes all white or opaque white, as in walleyed pike (named for the whites of its eyes). From the Anglo Saxon word for "beam" and by extension the disease "beam-in-the-eye," or blinded and clouded by a stick in the eye. Backwoods men often suffered from blindness from chasing game or fleeing enemies through thick brush and taking a twig in the eye.

were-: the prefix were is used in words like werewolf, werecat, etc. to mean that the creature can change back and forth from human to animal, or that the creature is half human and half animal. The prefix comes from the Anglo-Saxon word *wer*, meaning "man," so wolfman, catman, etc., work well as synonyms. Gypsies call these creatures man-into-wolf, man-into-cat, etc., and say the change is effected by a somersault. Medieval superstition attributed the change to incantations, such as the simple *"In canis corpore transmuto"* (Latin: "I change to the body of a dog"). Ozark superstition attributes such changes to American Indian belief structures, Gypsy magic, or the use of spells (incantations) and herbs (burned, chewed, eaten, etc.). Spells are often referred to as "remedies."

you'uns: phonetic spelling of you-ones, the Ozark plural of "you." We'uns (we-ones) and young'uns (young ones) are also heard in the same way "loved ones" is used by speakers of standard English.

Notes

All the stories in this anthology were heard and learned by the editors in a storytelling setting. The references to other books in which these stories appear are provided for readers interested in comparative study. Most of these stories were learned by these editors long before this anthology was envisioned, and therefore some lack exact dates and sources. As storytellers we often tell, and have recorded here, versions of stories distilled from many sources collected over a period of decades for which no single source can be cited. We have referred to existing variants when we have been aware of them, and cited our informants when it was possible.

In addition to the specific informants named in the Notes, the editors wish to thank Velma Mulkey, Roy Whiteleather, Clayton Beale, Ott Teague, Jim and Velma Bass, Ed Streng, D.A. Calloway, Troy Holt, and other Stone and Taney County natives, living and deceased, who welcomed these Texas and Oklahoma hillfolk to the Ozarks and spun their yarns for us.

In the notes that follow, full bibliographic information is provided for those books that are cited only once; bibliographic information for books cited more than once can be found in the Bibliography on page 189.

1. **OLD RAW HEAD** is the most common scary story in the Ozarks, and is regarded by many Ozarkers as the definitive Ozark ghost story. We, the editors, have heard this story from dozens of informants since 1969, but special thanks are due to Jo Anne Sears Rife (1975), Teresa Pijoan (1988), and Virginia Kirby Nickels of Harrison, Arkansas (1990). See *Ozark Superstitions*, pp. 235, 228, *Ghost Stories from the American Southwest*, p. 53, and *Favorite Scary Stories of American Children*, p. 11.

2. **RAW HEAD AND BLOODY BONES II** is also known among African-

American storytellers as "Little John Number Eight" (*'Ti' Huit Jean* in Creole French). This variant is told alongside the traditional Ozark variant (story no. 1 in this collection). Teresa Pijoan (1988) and Jackie Torrence (1991) contributed to this variant, as well as teen and preteen African-American story listeners we have met. See *Ozark Superstitions*, p. 236.

3. **THE WOMAN IN THE BED** has been told to us numerous times, with varying details. Steve Baldwin of Miller, Missouri, told one version in 1966. See *The Devil's Pretty Daughter*, p. 69.

4. **PENNYWINKLE! PENNYWINKLE!** is an Ozark variant of Grimms' "The Juniper Tree," which appears in fragmentary form in *Who Blowed Up the Church House?* p. 53. John C. Goldsberry of Schooner Creek (Stone County), Missouri, contributed to this retelling in 1980. See also *Ozark Superstitions*, p. 236, and Randolph's *Ozark Ghost Stories*, p. 23.

5. **BLOOD-RED CEDAR** is another Ozark variant of Grimms' "The Juniper Tree" (see story no. 4) contributed to in part by Bruce Grimes (1982) and Ken Haines (1979), both of Stone County, Missouri. While the song varies from version to version, ours is sung to "The Ash Grove." See also *Who Blowed Up the Church House?* p. 53, and *Favorite Scary Stories of American Children*, p. 78.

6. **BLOOD IN THE ROOT CELLAR** is an allegory for the onset of menstruation as much as it is a horror story. "Granny" (Reba) Flowers of Oak Grove, Arkansas, provided us with the basis of this retelling in 1981. See *The Talking Turtle*, p. 5.

7. **THE DUMB SUPPER** is a common Ozark folk practice and related folktale. Steven Milo Carter of Republic, Missouri, and "Silky" (Lynn) Baldwin of Reeds Spring, Missouri, provided versions between 1978 and 1983, but this variant is the one told by Thomas Phillips of Hot Springs, Arkansas, in 1976, told as the truth in his family. See also *Who Blowed Up the Church House?* p. 22, and *Ozark Country*, p. 140.

8. **RACHEL AND THE GOLDEN COINS** is a common Ozark and Southern folktale. For the African-American variant, see *African-American Folktales* (Little Rock: August House, 1993, p. 32), collected in Jackson, Mississippi. This Ozark variant often deals with a Jewish ghost giving his money to a Jewish girl named Rachel, but that element is missing from this version, given to us in part by Lloyd "Shad" Heller of Indian Point (Stone County), Missouri, in about 1981. See also *Sticks in the Knapsack*, p. 15, and Randolph's *Ozark Ghost Stories*, p. 9.

9. **FINGER BONES** is told in many variants (see *Ozark Superstitions*, p. 238), but this is the version told to us by Luther Taylor in 1980. See "Finger Bones" in *American Folk Tales and Songs* by Richard Chase (New York: New American Library of World Literature, 1956, pp.60-63).

10. **VANISHING RIDER** is the best known Ozark ghost story, a hill version of the best known urban legend, "The Vanishing Hitchhiker." This variant has been told around Mountain Home, Arkansas, for almost a century. We have heard this story too many times to credit a single source. See also *The Devil's Pretty Daughter*, p. 79.

11. **PETIT JEAN** is perhaps the best known ghost story in Central Arkansas and the Ouachita mountains. It has endless variations, but this version was told to us by Robert A. Aprea, then of Russellville, Arkansas, in 1987. See also *Folklore of Romantic Arkansas I*, p. 193.

12. **MARY CALHOUN** is the Ozark variant of the Irish folktale "Mary Culhane and the Dead Man." We have heard this story in fragments and reconstructed this variant from scary stories told in Catholic families. See also *Ozark Tall Tales*, p. 111, *Ghost Stories from the American Southwest*, p. 143, and *The Goblins Giggle* by Molly Bang (Gloucester: Peter Smith, 1988, p. 29).

13. **THE MO MO** is the latest version (1970s-1980s) of the traditional Ozark monster sometimes described as being golden-furred (the 1940s) and blue-furred (the 1920s). *Springfield News-leader* columnist Alanson Haswell wrote of the Blue Man being seen near Springfield in the 1920s, as related to us by his grandson, Robert Haswell. A similar creature inhabits Nob Hill, Arkansas (see story no. 17), and has been seen in the Ouachitas (see *Ozark Country*, p. 313). Steven Milo Carter of Stone County, Missouri, told us this story in 1988.

14. **SMOKEY JOE** is one of the two well known and well loved Boy Scout urban legends surrounding the Buffalo River area of Newton County, Arkansas, and Camp Orr. Greg Ferguson (1960s), Jeff Corr Richardson (1980s), Lee Fisher, and Ronnie Brown (1970s) all contributed details to this story, which first entered print in *Ozark Tall Tales*, p. 128. See also story no. 18.

15a. **THE OLD BLACK BOOGER I** is a well known Ozark scary story with narrative and "jump" variants. Ken Holt of Coon Ridge, Missouri, provided a fragment in 1979. A similar event takes place in the longer Scandinavian folktale, "The Boy Who Went Out to Learn Fear." See also *The Talking Turtle*, p. 22.

THE OLD BLACK BOOGER jump variant footnoted on page 72 is told just like the standard story, but on the last line the teller jumps from his rocking chair and grabs the nearest child listener. In the traditional Ozark jump storytelling, kids who know a certain story move away from the teller and encourage kids who don't know the story to sit close to the teller. At the "jump," the victims get the thrill of fear, and the "old hands" get the amusement of watching the victims' reactions. See also *The Talking Turtle*, p. 22.

15b. **THE OLD BLACK BOOGER—II** song variant is completely different from the folktale variant . The booger in this song is blackhearted, or a *blackguard*, and a foreign soldier being quartered in a home against the homeowner's wishes. The original probably was about English soldiers in Ireland, changed to British soldiers in the Thirteen Colonies, then moved to Union soldiers in Confederate sympathizer's homes. Many tunes and verses exist, but this version ends with a goul reference that makes it sometimes sung at scary story sessions. Edith Fulton Stone of Galena, Missouri, gave us the basis for this song. See *Ozark Folksongs* v. 1, p. 291; also see *Songs of the Ozark Folk* by Rainey, Leo, et al (Branson: The Ozarks Mountaineer, 1972, p. 6).

16. **THE "MAY NEVER ARRIVE"** ghost caboose story was told around Eureka Springs, Arkansas, in the 1950s and around Harrison, Arkansas, in the 1940s. Sightings were attributed to hobos of questionable drinking habits. Dr. Henry V. Kirby of Harrison, Arkansas, provided this variant in the 1980s. Dr. Kirby was the grandson of the Leonidas Kirby mentioned in the story. See also *Ozark Tales and Superstitions*, p. 24.

17. **THE BOOGER UNDER NOB HILL** was told in Siloam Springs, Arkansas, between 1963 and 1965, always having happened to a friend of a friend in the Springdale area (twenty miles away, a favorite Saturday night trip). The story resembles the "orance cat" or "wompus cat" with golden fur seen around Reeds Spring, Missouri, in the Abesville area in the 1950s, and the blue-furred wild man reported east and south of Springfield, Missouri, in the 1920s. See also *We Always Lie to Strangers*, p. 56, *Ozark Country*, p. 313, and *Ozark Tales and Superstitions*, p. 21.

18. **THE CREATURE IN THE HOLE** is a popular title given to more than one story. (See *Ghost Stories from the American Southwest*, p. 137, for the central Arkansas variant, *Ozark Tall Tales*, p. 121, for the north Arkansas variant.) The monster in the White River at Newport, Arkansas, is also sometimes called by this name and is generally explained as an alligator, a huge gar, or the result of too many sixpacks on a hot night. Lee Fisher of Harrison, Arkansas, and Ron Brown of Springfield, Missouri, provided this variant in

the 1980s. This is the second of two very popular Boy Scout camp stories in Northern Arkansas (see story no. 14).

19. **OLD WALLEYES** is rarely told anymore, supplanted by the more popular gower or gowrow or gowerow (see story no. 21 and *Ozark Tall Tales*, p. 21). The name refers to the clouded, staring eyes associated with the creature, which may be based on a blind wildcat of enormous proportions. There is a strong thematic resemblance between this story and one about a panther chasing a wagon with a mother and her baby in it, which leads us to the wildcat conjecture. Wilford Haymes of Elkton (Webster County), Missouri, provided the basis for this retelling. See also *The Devil's Pretty Daughter*, p. 11, "Old Walleyes" in the Glossary, and "Baby Hungry" in *I'll Tell You a Tale* (Boston: Little, Brown & Co., 1960, p. 209).

20. **JACK AND THE SALLY-BALLY** was told to us in the summer of 1985 by an Ozark family whose name we never learned. The story had been told in their family for generations, and embroidered by the tellers. (In the original variant they told, the Sally-Bally had one of its hands in the shape of a toilet seat!) The telling element in the name may be the low shrubs that grow over the creature. Low willows called sallee or sally in English were called *sealh* in Anglo-Saxon, and could give rise to the creature's name. Vance Randolph collected a variant called "Sally Bally Cato." See also "Bally Sally Cato" in *Legends and Lore of Missouri* (San Antonio: The Naylor Co., 1951, p. 68).

21. **THE GOWEROW IN MARVEL CAVE** was told to us by Lloyd "Shad" Heller of Indian Point (Stone County), Missouri, in 1979. The same story is told as happening near Harrison, Arkansas, in *We Always Lie to Strangers*, p. 44. See "gowerow" in the Glossary, *The Talking Turtle*, p. 55, and *Ozarks Country*, p. 54.

22. **THE BOOGER DOG** is told in countless variants in Stone and Taney counties. (See *Ozark Superstitions*, p. 224, *The Talking Turtle*, p. 74, and Randolph's *Ozark Ghost Stories*, p. 23.) The booger dog is sometimes unkillable, but usually oversized and out-of-place (see Glossary), and usually possessed of some preternatural property (e.g. headless, eyeless, leaving no footprints in the snow, capable of speech, etc.). Stories include such elements as "the dog paced the victim, just off the road," "the dog passed the victim on the run, then was waiting for him around the bend," and "I saw the dog, but I was too young to realize that dogs don't get as big as cows."

23. **THE BOOGER CATS** is perhaps the second most often told story of this genre. The boogers are sometimes demons or monsters, always carnivorous in appearance, and the repeated line of speech is often "Is

it time yet?" instead of "shall we start?" Interestingly, the creature awaited is almost always named Martin, regardless of its genus, perhaps due to the association with martin or marten, the *mustela americana*, a weasel-like pine marten of supposedly voracious carnivorous appetite. See *We Always Lie to Strangers*, p. 56, *Who Blowed Up the Church House?* p. 163, and "Booger Cat" in *A Treasury of Southern Folklore* by B.A. Botkin (New York: Crown Publishers, 1949, pp. 438-39).

24. THE CAT'S PAW is another often told story with seemingly infinite variants about a witch discovered while in her were-state (see Glossary). In the morning, horseshoes are found nailed on the hands of an evil witch woman. In other variants, something (even a severed part of the witch's were-anatomy) is thrown in an oven and the witch keeps coming over to borrow some household item or provision to break the spell that connects her to the now-burning part, which is causing her immense pain. Janice Duley of Leslie, Arkansas, told us this one in 1990. See *Ozark Country*, p. 164, *The Talking Turtle*, p. 174, and *Ozarks Country*, p. 60.

25. THE CAT KING was told to us by an unidentified "local" (see Glossary) in 1979. It is an excellent example of Ozark humor, lost on most non-Ozark readers, that always makes the hillfolks laugh. Cats are often associated with witchcraft and were-animal manifestations (see Glossary) and are often given the power of speech in stories. See *Who Blowed Up the Church House?* p. 40, and *Ozark Superstitions*, p. 236.

26. SHE'S GOT ME! is told as a favorite rural urban legend, very often sworn to as the truth among Ozark teens. One variant told in Harrison, Arkansas, involves a Scout knife through the cuff of a pair of Boy Scout uniform pants. This version came from Tom Phillips of Hot Springs, Arkansas, in the Ouachitas. For a Mexican version, see *Folktales of Mexico* (Chicago: University of Chicago Press, 1970, p. 166, #61b); for a Georgia variant see *Storytellers* (Athens: University of Georgia Press, 1989, p. 325).

27. WHO'S FOLLOWING ME? is another rural urban legend told commonly in the Ozarks by teens and preteens, often sworn to as the truth. One variant has a group of Halloweeners (see Glossary) trick or treating, supposedly chased (or sometimes actually followed by a sinister man who turns out to be the father of one of them, following to protect them). See *Favorite Scary Stories of American Children*, p. 57.

28. RED VELVET RIBBON in this variant was told to us by Lydia Rees in the late 1980s, when she was a preteen. This is a very old story, first

anthologized by Washington Irving, and known by many names such as "The Red Thread," "The Yellow Ribbon," etc., in England.

29. **THE HEADLESS FOREIGNER** is told around Galena, Missouri, and in Taney County. Lloyd "Shad" Heller told a fragment of this along with his "Wilderness Road" story in the 1980s. See *The Talking Turtle*, p. 9.

30. **THE HEADLESS BRAKEMAN** was told to us by Michael Olin Poe at Fayetteville, Arkansas, in 1967. Although the events took place near Crossett, Arkansas, the story is very popular in the Ozarks, especially among the college-age community at the University of Arkansas in Fayetteville. See *Ghost Stories from the American Southwest*, p. 41.

31. **THE SENATH LIGHT** was first told by Tom Phillips while he was a student at Arkansas State University in Jonesboro in 1976. Mr. Phillips suggests the nearby New Madrid Fault may somehow cause the lights. (August 5, 1990). See *Ghost Stories from the American Southwest*, p. 44.

32. **THE MIAMI LIGHT** was told to us by Katie Wamser and others from northeast Oklahoma in July 1989. Local mining operations or the nearby Hornet Light may be the cause. See also *Ghost Stories from the American Southwest*, p. 48.

33. **THE HORNET LIGHT** is told throughout the Ozarks in numerous variants. Often called the Devil's Promenade, fragments from eyewitnesses David Allen Woolly, Richard Alan Young, Don Kenney, Michael Olin Poe, Henry Klussman, and many others embellish this "standard" version of the origin of the light. See *Ozark Superstitions*, p. 233, for Randolph's comments. See also *The Talking Turtle*, p. 174, *Ghost Stories from the American Southwest*, p. 48, and *Ozark Country*, p. 160.

34. **THE HORNET BURIAL GROUND** is one explanation for the Spook Light at Hornet, collected from Johnny Brewer of Grove, Oklahoma, in August 1989. See *Ghost Stories from the American Southwest*, p. 49, and *Ozark Superstitions*, p. 234.

35. **THE SPLIT HORNET LIGHT** is the only story of all those we've heard about the Spook Light at Hornet in which the light splits. Told to us by Betty Gresham of Stone County, Missouri, in October 1990. See *Ghost Stories from the American Southwest*, p. 49, and *Ozark Superstitions*, p. 234.

36. **THE STILL HORNET LIGHT** was told to us by Bill Frenchman from Disney, Oklahoma, in August of 1989. Just as the Spook Light was a favorite weekend road trip for University of Arkansas students in

the 1960s, it was a draw for high schoolers from Oklahoma in the 1940s and 1950s. See *Ghost Stories from the American Southwest,* p. 49.

37. **THE BABY IN THE BACK ROOM** was told to us in June 1990 by Kathryn Cavert who lived in Newton County, Arkansas, in the 1960s. The crying baby motif is the most common ghostly noise, and is most often explained away (adequately or not) by wind in isolated areas. Similar events occur in Vance Randolph's *Ozark Ghost Stories,* p. 18.

38. **THE BABY IN THE CAVE** was told to us by Patricia Smith from Harrison, Arkansas, in June 1990. Similar events occur in Vance Randolph's *Ozark Ghost Stories,* p. 18.

39. **THE GHOST AT BOBO** was told by Chuck Wakely during the summer of 1990.

40. **THE GHOST IN THE CHURCH** was told at a storytelling session in Harrison, Arkansas, at Halloween, 1987, by a teenager who asked not to be identified. He may have visited the same building referred to in *Ozark Superstitions,* p. 218, at Oak Grove, Arkansas.

41. **THE GHOST OF FLOYD EDINGS** has been heard by these editors many times. This version and the accompanying ballad were given to us by local folklore enthusiast JoAnne Sears Rife of Harrison, Arkansas, in the late 1960s and again in the early 1970s. Lines 9-10 of this ballad version are rare, supplying a lacuna in other variants that strand Floyd in Berryville at the end of line 8. "Come" is the past participle used as the past tense of "came"; "nigh" is an archaic word meaning "near," and "plaguèd" is an old form of "plaguey" or "troublesome." The last two lines of this version are sometimes left off, omitting the detail of the blanket. The ghostly dictation was suggested by another informant. See another variant in *Ozark Tales and Superstitions,* p. 50.

42. **THE GRINNING GHOST** was provided on October 18, 1990, by John C. Brosam and Patricia Mertz of Kansas City, to whom the incident happened.

43. **THE GHOST PLAYS POOL** was told by Janet Shaw on June 11, 1990. She lived in the house—but not for long! See *Ghost Stories from the American Southwest,* p. 78.

44. **THE GHOST ON THE THIRD FLOOR** was told to us on August 6, 1990, by Thomas Phillips, who once worked at Harding College. See *Ghost Stories from the American Southwest,* p. 94.

45. **THE GHOST OF ELLA BARHAM** was told by George White, a member of the jury who hanged Odus Davidson, to his granddaughter Pat

Greeson of Harrison, Arkansas, who conveyed it to us June 11, 1990. See *Ghost Stories from the American Southwest*, p. 98.

46. **FROZEN CHARLOTTE** seems to be a romantic ballad of the late 1800s that became a folktale (see *Ozark Folksongs* IV-105 for an explanation and a set of variants including "Sharlotty" or "Young Charlottie"). It is also possible that real events in post-Civil War Mountain Home, Arkansas, may have caused the event to take the name of the ballad. Judy Domeny, folksinger from Rogersville, Missouri, provided some of the details of this retelling. See also Rainey, Leo, et al. *Songs of the Ozark Folk* (Branson, Missouri: *The Ozarks Mountaineer*, 1972), p. 38.

47. **THE LEGEND OF VIVIA THOMAS** has been heard all her life by Judy Dockrey Young, formerly of Wagoner, Oklahoma. See another version in *Ozark Tales and Superstitions*, p. 65.

48. **I CAN'T GET IN!** is a family story from a teenager of Newton County, Arkansas, who asked not to be identified, told at Harrison in the 1970s. As soon as he heard the story in his childhood, the informant asked, but he was too late; the man who actually saw the skeleton was already deceased and no more details could be obtained. See *Ghost Stories from the American Southwest*, p. 29.

49. **STILL ON PATROL** is commonly told in south central Missouri, especially in Greene, Christian, and Stone Counties. We heard it prior to January 1, 1989, at Silver Dollar City.

50. **THE BURNING BRIDE** was first heard by Richard Alan Young between 1968 and 1969 in Fayetteville, Arkansas, while living at 355 Fletcher Street on East Mountain. The story was circulated in the "Tin Cup" neighborhood in many variants. A different variant appears in *Ozark Tales and Superstitions*, p. 17. This story was popular in the African-American community, but appeared to be told as amusement only.

51. **THE FIDDLER IN FARALONE CAVE** is found in *The Talking Turtle*, p. 27, and is told in many variants associated with many caves. We first heard it associated with Cobb Cave at Lost Valley (now a state park) in Newton County, Arkansas, with the fiddler being in Eden Falls Cave above it. Ghostly sounds are often associated with caves, and have two general explanations: lost babies and fiddler's ghosts. No single source can be cited for this story. See *Ozarks Country*, p. 180, and Vance Randolph's *Ozark Ghost Stories*, p. 7. The story is told mostly in Howell, Stone, and Taney Counties in Missouri, wherein no cave has either name, although Bear Den Cave (now under Table Rock Lake) has been suggested as the site.

52. THE GHOST IS STILL MAD appears in *The Talking Turtle*, p. 59, although in that variant the protagonist is named Forrest. See also *Ozark Superstitions*, p. 222. Either this story "gets around" or there are a lot of angry revenants in the Ozarks. We first heard it as having happened in Stone County, Missouri, near Yokum's Pond (around Reeds Spring) from an unidentified informant in 1978. (The Yoachims or Yoakums were the first European inhabitants of the area.)

53. THE GHOST AT VIRGIN'S BLUFF is a romanticized, Westernized story that may have had origins in fact. Grislier versions are found in *The Devil's Pretty Daughter*, p. 51, *Ozark Superstitions*, pp. 217-18, *Ozark Country*, pp. 304-306, and a similar version can be found in *Ozark Tales and Superstitions*, p.27. See also "The Indian Chieftain's Curse," *The Sunday News & Leader* (Springfield, Missouri) November 23, 1958, and *The Press* (Springfield, Missouri) December 15, 1930 (Floyd Sullivan, informant).

54. THE GHOST DOOR was collected prior to January 1, 1989, from a teenaged informant (who is not the source of any other story in this collection). See *Ghost Stories from the American Southwest*, p. 68. A door used by a ghost is a common motif in Ozark lore; see *Ghost Stories from the American Southwest*, p. 22, for an account of Anglo-Saxon ghost beliefs surviving in Newton County, Arkansas, and *Ozark Superstitions*, p. 215, for a similar motif.

55. THE GHOST AT HUGHES is also found in *Ghost Stories from the American Southwest*, p. 69, collected from Tom Phillips of Hot Springs, August 5, 1990. He heard the story from the family involved (whose name the editors have withheld) whose sons were his fraternity brothers at Arkansas State University in Jonesboro in the 1970s.

56. THE GHOST AT GINGER BLUE was heard in teenage years by Richard Alan Young while visiting Ginger Blue, Missouri. Alternate versions appear in *Ozark Folksongs II*, p. 385, and *Ozark Tales and Superstitions*, p. 29. Sometimes there is no ghost; sometimes the maiden dies at the cave mouth.

57. THE GHOST AT THE CONFEDERATE GRAVEYARD was told by the late Dr. Ben Kimpel, the skeptical next-door resident to the cemetery, who did not believe the stories, although some other neighbors did. Interestingly enough, recent whispered rumors suggest the Confederate cemetery is more of a monument, with few actual remains. The graves outside the woods are definitely real, however. The ghost is seen outside the cemetery, near the graves of local folk, long neglected in the woods that have grown up in the twentieth

century. We first heard this story in the early 1960s at the University of Arkansas.

58. **THE GHOST OF NICKERSON RIDGE** is very close to these editors, literally, because the ghost haunted the ridge on which we reside. (see Nickerson Ridge in the Glossary.) Otto Ernest Rayburn introduced Vance Randolph to Tomp Turner in July 1932, at which time Tomp told of the 1915 sighting of the headless ghost. See *Ozark Superstitions*, p. 228, *Ozark Country*, p. 310, and Vance Randolph's *Ozark Ghost Stories*, p. 16. Some residents called the ghost/creature Old Raw Head, but that seems to be a recent name change. At least one teller claimed it was the ghost of Alf Bolen (or Bolin or Bolden). See *The Devil's Pretty Daughter*, p. 137, and *Outlaw Tales*, p. 148. The ghost is one of the best known in the Ozarks, seen "since pioneer times." Randolph could not find a murder account or other explanation for the ghost, which (to believers) would only mean that the instigating event occurred before 1802 and the arrival of English-speaking settlers. The ghost has been seen less since the 1915 sighting, and according to some accounts, not at all since the impounding of Table Rock Lake in 1959.

59. **THE CORPSE RISES AGAIN** is a version of "Grave Robbers" in *The Devil's Pretty Daughter*, p. 24. This is a very common "joke" in English-speaking folklore, and not unique to the Ozarks. We have heard it many times. See also *Ozark Superstitions*, p. 214.

60. **SKIN-AND-BONES** is a jump song, sung with a scream at the end to frighten young listeners, heard by Jo Anne Sears Rife in her childhood in Bentonville, Arkansas. See *Ghost Stories from the American Southwest*, p. 31, and *Ozark Folksongs I*, p. 301.

61. **IT'S COLD IN THE GRAVE** is another common "joke" not peculiar to the Ozarks. Lewin Hayden Dockrey told this one at Rescue, Missouri, in the 1960s. See *Hot Springs and Hell*, p. 94.

62. **YOU CAN'T GET OUT!** is told around the Ozarks, but we first heard it in Texas in the 1950s from Dr. Homer Harry Young. It is also well known in Oklahoma. See *Ghost Stories from the American Southwest*, p. 28, and *Hot Springs and Hell*, p. 8.

63. **STEALING PAWPAWS** is also called "The Pawpaw Lie" (See "lie" in the Glossary), and was the favorite joke of Judy Dockrey Young's father, Lewin Hayden Dockrey, late of Rescue, Missouri, told in the 1960s. (See also pawpaw in the Glossary.) See *Ghost Stories from the American Southwest*, p. 27, and "Dividing the Dead," in *Who Blowed Up the Church House?* p. 83. See also *Ozark Superstitions*, p. 212.

64. **THE RED LIGHT** is found also in *Ghost Stories from the American Southwest*, p. 44. Collected by Tom Phillips from Bobby Box in Jonesboro, Arkansas, in the 1970s and given to us August 6, 1990. Mr. Phillips swears he knew college students at Arkansas State University who "fell for" the light, either not noticing the radio tower light or failing to make the mental connection.

65. **THE HAINTED CAR** is also called "The Haunted Car." It first entered print in our *Ozark Tall Tales*, p. 118 (see also *Ghost Stories from the American Southwest*, p. 29). Dr. Morgan Martin Young told this joke around Siloam Springs, Arkansas, in the 1960s. He was the father of Richard Alan Young, and it was his favorite story.

Bibliography

Allsopp, Fred. *Folklore of Romantic Arkansas* (in two volumes) (New York: Duell, Sloan, & Pearce, 1941).

Deane, Ernie. *Ozarks Country* (Branson, Missouri: The Ozarks Mountaineer, 1975).

Randolph, Vance. *The Devil's Pretty Daughter and Other Ozark Folk Tales* (New York: Columbia University Press, 1955).

_____. *Down in the Holler* (Norman: University of Oklahoma Press, 1953).

_____. *Ozark Ghost Sories* (Girard, Kansas: Haldeman-Julius Publications, c. 1944).

_____. *Ozark Superstitions* (New York: Columbia University Press, 1947).

_____. *Sticks in the Knapsack* (New York: Columbia University Press, 1958).

_____. *The Talking Turtle and Other Ozark Folk Tales* (New York: Columbia University Press, 1957).

_____. *Who Blowed Up the Church House? and Other Ozark Folk Tales* (New York: Columbia University Press, 1952).

_____. *We Always Lie to Strangers* (New York, Columbia University Press, 1951).

Rayburn, Otto Ernest. *Ozark Country* (New York: Duell, Sloan & Pearce, 1941).

Steele, Phillip W. *Ozark Tales and Superstitions* (Gretna, Lousiana: Pelican Publishing Company, 1983).

Young, Richard and Judy Dockrey. *Favorite Scary Stories of American Children* (Little Rock: August House, 1990).

_____. *Ghost Stories from the American Southwest* (Little Rock: August House, 1991).

_____. *Ozark Tall Tales* (Little Rock August House, 1989).

_____. *Outlaw Tales* (Little Rock: August House, 1992).

Other Books and Audiocassettes from August House Publishers

Race with Buffalo

and Other Native American Stories for Young Readers

Collected by Richard and Judy Dockrey Young

Hardback $19.95 / ISBN 0-87483-343-4
Paperback $9.95 / ISBN 0-87483-342-6

Listening for the Crack of Dawn

Donald Davis

Winner of the Anne Izard Storyteller's Choice Award

Hardback $17.95 / ISBN 0-87483-153-9
Paperback $11.95 / ISBN 0-87483-130-X
Double Audiobook $18.00 / ISBN 0-87483-147-4

Once Upon a Galaxy

The ancient stories that inspired Star Wars, Superman,
and other popular fantasies

Josepha Sherman

Hardback $19.95 / ISBN 0-87483-386-8
Paperback $11.95 / ISBN 0-87483-387-6

Eleven Turtle Tales

Adventure Tales from Around the World

Pleasant DeSpain

Hardback $12.95 / ISBN 0-87483-388-4

AUGUST HOUSE PUBLISHERS, INC.
P.O. BOX 3223
LITTLE ROCK, AR 72203
1-800-284-8784